Return to Life

DINA DAVIDOVICH

DENA ARYEH
PUBLISHING

LOS ANGELES, CALIFORNIA

Published by:
Dena Aryeh Publishing
11726 San Vicente Bl., Suite 560
Los Angeles, CA 90049

Email: Dena@returntolifebook.com
Website: http://returntolifebook.com/

Project Manager: Marla Markman, MarlaMarkman.com
Cover Illustration: Irina Filcer, IrinaFilcer.com
Cover Design and Interior Design: Kelly Cleary, kellymaureencleary@gmail.com
Editor: Tammy Ditmore, https://editmore.com/

Publisher's Cataloging-in-Publication Data

Names: Davidovich, Dina, author.

Title: Return to life / Dina Davidovich.

Description: Los Angeles, CA: Return to Life Publishing LLC, 2025.

Identifiers: LCCN: 2024907511 I ISBN: 979-8-9904358-0-3 (paperback) I
979-8-9904358-1-0 (ebook)

Subjects: LCSH Davidovich, Dina. I Holocaust, Jewish (1939-1945)--Hungary--
Personal narratives. I Jews--Hungary--Biography. I Jewish children in the
Holocaust--Hungary--Biography. I Holocaust survivors--Biography. I Auschwitz
(Concentration camp)--Personal narratives. I BISAC BIOGRAPHY &
AUTOBIOGRAPHY / Memoirs I BIOGRAPHY & AUTOBIOGRAPHY / Historical
I HISTORY / Modern / 20th Century / Holocaust

Classification: LCC DS135.H93 D38 2025 I DDC 940.53/180922--dc23

979-8-9904358-0-3 (Print)
979-8-9904358-1-0 (Ebook)

Printed in the United States of America

To the memory of my parents.

*To the memory of the many millions of innocents
killed in the greatest holocaust in history.*

*To my children, in order that they may know
my life and never forget it.*

*To the whole of humanity, in order that it may defend
the weak against torturers and assassins.*

Table of Contents

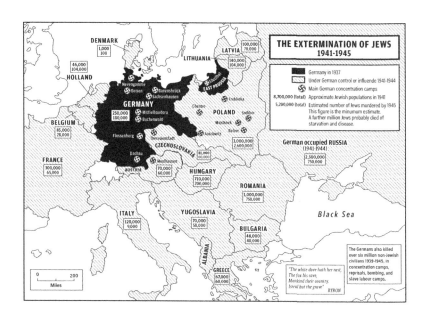

THE EXTERMINATION OF JEWS
1941-1945

▰ Germany in 1937

▱ Under German control or influence 1941-1944

✺ Main German concentration camps

8,700,000 (total) Approximate Jewish populations in 1941

5,200,000 (total) Estimated number of Jews murdered by 1945
This figure is the minimum estimate.
A further million Jews probably died of
starvation and disease.

DENMARK
1,000
100

HOLLAND
46,000
104,000

LATVIA
100,000
70,000
140,000
104,000

LITHUANIA

EAST PRUSSIA

Nevengamme
Beisen
Ravensbrück
Sachsenhausen

GERMANY
250,000
180,000
Mittielhaudora
Buchenwald

Chelmo
Treblinka
POLAND
Sobibor
Majdanek
Belzec
Auschwitz
3,000,000
2,600,000

BELGIUM
85,000
28,000

Flossenberg
Theresienstadt
CZECHOSLOVAKIA
81,000
60,000

German occupied RUSSIA
(1941-1944)
2,500,000
750,000

FRANCE
300,000
65,000

Dachau
AUSTRIA
Mauthausen
70,000
60,000

HUNGARY
710,000
200,000

ROMANIA
1,000,000
750,000

Black Sea

ITALY
120,000
9,000

YUGOSLAVIA
70,000
58,000

BULGARIA
48,000
40,000

ALBANIA

GREECE
67,000
60,000

0   200
Miles

The Germans also killed
over six million non-Jewish
civilians 1939-1945, in
concentration camps,
reprisals, bombing, and
slave labour camps.

"The white dove hath her nest,
The fox his cave,
Mankind their country,
Isreal but the grave."
BYRON

PROLOGUE

THIS BOOK TELLS THE STORY of the saddest and most terrible year of my life—the year my family, like millions of other European families, fell victim to the heavy-handed barbarity of the Nazis. This is a true story; everything in it is authentic: my childhood, my family, my native village in Hungary. When I was thirteen years of age I was taken prisoner, in the midst of a storm of evil and fanaticism, by someone who believed they were of a superior race and, for a time, managed to subjugate Europe. I tell here of the year I spent in concentration camps and the sufferings to which I was subjected. My survival was a miracle.

At the beginning, my idea was to write a testament exclusively for my beloved children, in order for them to know the inferno I was thrown into by brutality, intolerance, and hate when I was just a child.

After finishing the manuscript, I showed it to my friend, the talented writer Dunia Wasserstrom, also a survivor of Auschwitz, who has published various works about the concentration camps.

After reading it, Dunia pointed out to me how important it was that these pages be rescued from oblivion and spread beyond the circle of my friends and family to a wider circle of readers. She convinced me that if every one of the survivors of the concentration camps would write the history of our tragic experience, we would help make sure such horrors never occur again.

I tell in my text, leaving nothing out, all the facts I remember of those tormented dark days. Each paragraph was written with absolute sincerity and with the greatest authenticity possible. If one of my memories was vague or confused, I chose to eliminate that story in order to be truthful.

I consider it important to begin my story with some unforgettable scenes of my happy childhood in my native village, before captivity, in order to offer the reader a vivid contrast between those enchanting times and the year of infamy to which I was subjected later.

On not a few occasions while writing of the happenings of that year which was—for me—a painful eternity, I felt as though a burning iron had buried itself in my heart, and tears came to my eyes as though those terrible deeds had taken place only yesterday.

I wish to acknowledge my gratitude to the writer Jorge Mejia Prieto, who helped me professionally to give the language of my book a clear structure.

This work will have fulfilled its purpose if those who have suffered horrors like those I describe, as well as the reader lucky enough never to have done so, feel the impulse to thank God three times every day for bread and roof received and for the incomparable gift of freedom.

Dina Davidovich

MAY 8

TODAY, MAY 8, 1985, the date on which I begin to write the story of the first sixteen years of my life, is exactly forty years since my liberation. On that day, before the dawn, a woman outside the hut suddenly called: "We are free, we are alone, there are no longer any Germans here!"

On hearing these words, no one moved. A devastating silence prevented us from reacting. Free? It was impossible to believe it! It seemed a joke, but the situation in which we found ourselves, more dead than alive, was not a joking matter.

May 8, 1945, between four and five in the morning. It was still dark and would not get light until around six. None of us dared to go outside the hut to confirm or reject the incredible news. The only response to the shouts declaring our freedom were harsh cries from other women: "You are a beast!" "Go and cheat your mother and go to sleep!" "Sleep would be better for you than the dirty water they give us for breakfast!"

Rough expressions like these were common among the women *häftling* (prisoners) who had been there longer and suffered more: the Poles.

The Hungarians, even after a year of being in the place, maintained a proud, unbreakable exterior. The French, after six months in the camp, spent their time singing and displaying an indomitable spirit, despite having witnessed the deaths of several of their companions.

Just four days earlier, on May 4, I had marked my fourteenth birthday. My sister Magdalena was fifteen years old. Our mother was also with us. We were imprisoned with some five hundred women of different European nationalities: Hungarian, French, Polish. I was the youngest of them all.

With much fear we looked timidly out of the door to see whether we were really free. Then we went out one by one, with the greatest caution, looking around on all sides. The dawn was breaking when we realized life was also beginning to dawn for us! At last we were coming out of the nightmare!

The first thing that occurred to us, hungry as we were, was to run toward the place where the food was kept with the idea of giving ourselves a feast. We eagerly broke in the door of the storehouse, only to receive a sad awakening: the Germans had taken everything, leaving only a barrel of mustard.

It wasn't long before we heard music in the distance; it was the Russians entering the city.

Approximately one and a half hours later, a man dressed in civilian clothes entered the concentration camp and shouted to us: "Come out of there at once; if not, you will die; the camp is full of dynamite and they are going to blow it up at six!"

This man, thanks to his good heart or to his desire to be a hero (we never knew which), saved our lives. His timely warning made us immediately abandon that horrible place where we had suffered so much, and to run to meet the Russian Army, seeking their protection in case the Germans reappeared. Before he withdrew, we asked that man the name of the city or village where we found ourselves. He told us, "Georgenthal."

A PEACEFUL CHILDHOOD IN A CHARMING PLACE

I WAS BORN IN HUNGARY, IN A SMALL VILLAGE called Szécsény, in the state of Nógrád. I can see with the eyes of my soul what my birthplace was like in the golden and unrecoverable years of my early life. A picturesque village, its main street led to a beautiful little square where a monument to independence had been erected.

I also remember the majestic and very old Catholic church that attracted summer visitors from the city who admired this veritable architectural jewel. In front was a pretty garden with benches where the local inhabitants sat to converse and to relax.

There was also another building as beautiful, old and admired as the Catholic church: the synagogue. It was so significant for me, with its garden full of flowers and a dense thicket of raspberry bushes on one side which separated it from the garden of my house.

Not far away from there ran the Ipoly River. If we swam across the river for two or three minutes, we would be in Losonc, a village of the neighboring country of Czechoslovakia.

We Hungarians and the Czechs got along very well. Many Hungarians of the region spoke Czech, and not a few Czechs spoke Hungarian.

The inhabitants of Szécsény were mostly traders or land owners who built their mansions next to them. Around the village—eight, nine, or ten kilometers away—were smaller peasant hamlets; we children used to walk or ride our bicycles there.

The country around my village was dreamlike, with fields of corn and wheat. During the month of May a tree we called *ongora* blooms in the countryside with small flowers that come out in bunches. Some are white, some purple, and others a pale lilac, giving an intoxicating scent. A small wildflower also appears at that time, red in color; the pipach grows among another kind of yellow flower, offering a lovely contrast.

Szécsény is in a grape-growing and wine-distilling region. Fruits and vegetables were cultivated in the little hamlets surrounding my village. Their inhabitants were profoundly linked to the land, like very real manifestations of Hungarian folklore. These peasants came into Szécsény to sell their products at the market that took place every Friday in one of the streets of our village. It was a wonder of animation, noise, and color.

The people of the village wore their finest clothes on Sundays and strolled around and around along the main street. The women were outstanding with their impressive show of materials and colors. The most elegant wore a skirt with a total of twenty-five pleats, multicolored and very tight at the waist, which made them look like open umbrellas when they walked. They wore white stockings and red slippers and close-fitting red or black waistcoats that had been lovingly embroidered. With all this and their wide-sleeved white blouses, they looked like queens. And they were: queens of elegance and beauty, as the beauty of Hungarians is proverbial.

The men wore very loose white shirts, black trousers and beautifully embroidered waistcoats which were also black. And very shiny black boots. Worthy of their beautiful and elegant women, the men also showed off their proud bearing and grace.

These wonderful men and women were happy playing their musical instruments and dancing, which they did in spontaneous festivals in the village square, as people circled around to admire them.

The music and dances of the Hungarian people are justifiably world famous, and in them vibrates the spirit of a passionate, happy, and romantic nation of dreamers.

There is a very lovely Hungarian song which I first heard in my childhood. It is called Sad Sunday, and only a violinist who is

Hungarian by birth is capable of playing its melody with all its haunting beauty.

Another spectacle worth seeing in my native village were the policemen. Their uniforms were very striking and the hats they wore, decorated with ostrich plumes, really impressive. Dressed in this ostentatious fashion, they took charge of keeping the peace in the peaceful town.

A Small Jewish Community

My family consisted of my father, my mother, two brothers, my sister, and myself, the youngest daughter. We lived at Profeta Street, Number 1, now called the Street of The Martyrs, a name change I will explain in the course of this story of my life.

We belonged to the small Jewish community in the village, consisting of some 480 people, including those who lived on the outskirts. Some members of this community dedicated themselves to agriculture, others to raising livestock or to a trade, and a few were professional people.

Most European Jews spoke Yiddish, a language made up of elements of German and Hebrew languages.

At that time, the second language of the country, after Hungarian, was German, and it was obligatory to learn German in school after kindergarten. My parents spoke German very well and also spoke Yiddish. But in the bosom of my family we always spoke Hungarian since we felt deeply Hungarian by nationality and Jewish because of our religion. Hungarian Jews were deeply incorporated into the culture and customs of Hungary.

Our Jewish community had a primary school and the synagogue, which was led by the rabbi and by my father, who was the *hazzan* (singer), and therefore entrusted with the religious Jewish chants and in charge of circumcising the newly born baby boys. He had a beautiful baritone voice, and people who were not Jews used to stop in front of the synagogue, enraptured, to listen to him. In addition to his occupations in the synagogue, my father gave classes in Hebrew history in the primary school.

My Generous Father

My father's name was Ignacio, and the name of my mother was Margit. Both were natives of Miskolc, the second most important city in Hungary and a lovely place, which I visited when I was a child when my parents took me to the house of my paternal grandfather. My father took part in the First World War under the flag of Hungary. He was wounded in battle and decorated by the government. When I was small I saw a photograph of him taken when he was very young. He looked very gallant and elegant with his army uniform and his decorations.

When my father and mother married, they went to live in Szécsény, where they had their four children. The eldest was Ernest, the second Eugene; then Magdalena came to the world, and, lastly, I was born.

Physically, Papa was a fine-featured man, with white skin, blond hair, a narrow build, and a very distinguished air, heightened by the small beard which outlined the lower part of his face. His blue eyes shone with sparkles of goodness and understanding. He always wore dark suits. As regards his nature, his main characteristic was his generosity. No one coming to our door in search of help left without receiving his assistance. And no day passed in my home when food was not served and clothes given to the poor.

My mother told my brothers and me with an understanding smile that "if I left all the money with your father we wouldn't have anything to eat, because he'd give it all away to the poor." A man of great internal discipline and completely disinterested in money, Papa delivered his whole salary to Mama. If he needed any money he would ask her for it humbly.

With the children, my father was both loving and strict; always full of affection for us, but firm in requiring compliance with our duties. He was so unaffected and lacking in pride that, when we were small, he would place the medals he had won on the floor and make them into a train so that we could play with them.

Everyone loved my father. I adored him. His affectionate smile, gestures, and words are unforgettable to me. I remember that he often said to me: "The most noble and true religion in this world is to love one's neighbor."

My Industrious Mother

My father and my mother were alike in many ways: goodness, customs, character, religious sentiments. However, my mother was not a woman who would go to synagogue at all hours. She was completely dedicated to the obligations inherent to the good Jewish mother, efficiently administering the home. She ensured that foods were not mixed, that the meals were kosher in accordance with the dietary laws of the Jewish code; and every Friday, when the sun set, she would light the traditional candles and pray to God for her family and for all humanity.

Mama was charitable, but, of course, less than my father, since she had to ensure that her family lacked nothing. So, as soon as she received my father's salary, she would separate different amounts in small envelopes for the different payments she had to make: food, clothing, the servant's wages, etc. Once the amounts had been placed in the envelopes, this money was untouchable for other uses, and on the first of every month she always paid all that she owed. For her, it was a matter of honor to always pay everything on time.

My mother worked very hard, but she did it all with love for her family and with a pleasure and a joy which made her day light and pleasant.

Mother was an extraordinary cook, and she knew all the secrets to delicious Hungarian cooking. She herself cured the cucumbers, prepared bottled fruits and jams, made cheese and butter of an excellent quality, made bread, and baked cakes. She cultivated radishes, tomatoes, onions, and dill, the herb used in Hungarian cooking, in the orchard of our home. She knew, of course, how to use the exact amount of paprika, the sweet red powder which gives dishes the Hungarian touch.

My mother raised hens and geese, feeding the geese with corn soaked in water until they grew and fattened to the maximum. When one of her geese grew so fat it could hardly walk, she killed it. Before cooking it, she took out its enormous liver and took it to the shop for them to weigh on the scales, verifying that it weighed a kilo. She then went proudly back home and fried the liver in its own fat. When cold it was delicious, and we ate it in sandwiches or in pieces of the enormous round loaves my mother baked.

She also raised ducks. Duck is eaten a lot in Hungary, but it also has to be fattened, because a thin duck has little meat and its flavor is not as good as that of the fat duck, which, when roasted, forms one of the masterworks of Hungarian culinary art. But delicacies such as duck and goose were reserved for great occasions. Our daily fare consisted of potato soup or spaghetti sprinkled with nuts and sugar. The noodles for the soup were also made by Mama, since no factories for these products existed in the region.

I loved eating pieces of bread spread with chicken fat or with butter and jam. My mother had an obsession about overfeeding us; nevertheless, my father, my brothers, and I were all thin. She was, though, a robust woman, a typical beauty of the country and of the time, where corporeal exuberance was an important attribute of feminine beauty.

A housewife with great talent for administering the family budget, a tireless worker and exemplary mother, Mama was also to be admired for her cheerfulness, her charitable spirit, and her faith in God. She often said to us: "God helps us, because we live on your father's salary and this salary allows us to live well and also help many poor people."

The Lively and Talkative Youngest Child

My brother Ernest, the first-born, was six years older than me. A boy with an excellent character and very marked religious sentiments, he felt responsible for his younger brother and sisters. His vocation was medicine, but he was not able to follow this career as he wanted because the growing Nazi influence and antisemitism in Europe meant that Jews were forbidden to enter preparatory school. Therefore, they were prohibited from entering university.

My other brother, Eugene, was a year younger than Ernest and thus five years older than me. In those years of my childhood he was a very bright boy who possessed an extraordinary ability to work with his hands.

Magdalena, my only sister, was one year older than me. Her nature was exceptionally peaceful. She was little attracted to household chores but passionately fond of reading and study. Since we were both girls and the difference in our age was so slight, we got along very well. We all formed a very united family, and our home life was really happy.

As for me, I was a skinny but strong child, small, with fine features similar to those of my father, and very blond hair. I had great confidence in myself and my nature was open, happy, and affectionate. Restless and a good observer, I watched how some farmer friends of ours milked their cows, and one day I managed to milk them myself without difficulty. From then on, I took part in the milking every Sunday.

There were two doctors in the village. The one with the highest prestige who was beloved by the people was named Doctor Daniel. He was also Jewish and was a good friend of my father's and had a beautiful house where his consulting office was installed. He was a bachelor, and it was rumored that he had many mistresses. Children are curious by nature and we children of the village used to watch the doctor's house, trying to discover who his mistresses were.

One day, Doctor Daniel caught me snooping around his house. Instead of being angry with me, he said with a kind and amused expression: "Just fancy, you who were born practically dead, because the birth was a difficult one and I had to take care of your mother, who was very ill. I didn't even look at you because you were purple and seemed lifeless, until you yelled. You've grown up to be a mischievous, lively, and talkative child, a real spark. Who would have thought it?"

And it was true that I was a very lively and talkative child, because I liked everyone and enjoyed talking with them.

I wish I had been able to keep a photograph which showed my sister and myself when we were five and four years old, respectively.

There was a splendid photographer in Szécsény who insisted that my mother allow him to take a photograph of her two daughters. Convinced, my mother had a woman who sewed for her make us two identical dresses, white with some little balls of navy blue, for our picture.

Whenever my mother passed by the street where the photographer had his studio, he would remind my mother about the photograph. She told him to be patient—the dresses which she wanted us to wear for the picture were not yet ready. When they were finally finished, they were beautiful. Mama took us to the photographer's studio wearing them, and he took a picture of us which everyone liked.

In it I was sitting down, with a little ball in my hands, while Magdalena stood beside me. At that time we both had short hair. I was never able to recover that photo, which was lost with so many other things in the hurricane of destruction, hatred, and barbarism.

My Candy-Loving Grandmother

When my maternal grandfather died, his wife, Teresa, left Miskolc and came to live with us. She was very pretty, with green eyes and dark skin, and we all loved her very much. My father adored her and she adored my father.

I remember she had a very sweet tooth and hid candies under her goosefeather pillow, afraid that my brothers would enter her bedroom at night and steal them.

When our grandmother became ill and couldn't reach down to wash her feet, we grandchildren took turns washing them for her on a tray. She appreciated this attention very much and, as a prize, would take the grandchild who had washed her feet that day to the store and buy him or her caramels. It was the best way to show us her gratitude because candies were, for her, the best possible delight in this world.

I was six years old when Grandmother died at eighty-two years of age, one very cold December morning at nine o'clock. I ran to the synagogue to tell Papa of the death of Grandmother, who had died in my mother's arms.

I felt Grandmother's death very strongly on that winter morning, when the snow was almost a meter high.

LIFE AMONG FLOWERS
AND FRUIT TREES

NOW LET ME TELL YOU what our house was like. It was a typical village house, only one story and made of stone. Ours was next to the synagogue and had a roomy living room and three bedrooms. One bedroom was occupied by my parents, another by my brothers, and the third by my maternal grandmother, my sister, and me.

The kitchen was largest room in the house, and it was the center of constant activity. That is where my mother baked, kneaded bread, made cakes, and prepared cheese and butter together with bottled fruits and jams. And on feast days she prepared the superb dishes of Hungarian haute cuisine.

On one side of the kitchen was an enormous room without windows that served as a natural refrigerator. There my mother stored the preserved fruits and jams, as well as cereals and miscellaneous foodstuffs, for winter. I will never forget the monumental table where my mother placed the cakes so that we wouldn't eat them outside mealtimes. We were not allowed to go into the cold room without her permission.

The garden in front of the house was a fiesta of exuberance, freshness, and color. Its originality and splendor were the work of my mother, who arranged it and took care of it personally, cutting the masses of flowers in different ways. One section was filled with red roses, another dahlias, still another chrysanthemums, giving the impression of hearts, cookies, etc., in accordance with the imagination and taste of Mama.

Moved by her love of gardening, she would get up at four in the morning and sit on the lawn with the maid, sifting dirt through her fingers in order to form the hillocks that she would then sow artistically with flowers. Dahlias of many sizes and colors were her favorites.

Just outside the kitchen door was the orchard with plum and other fruit trees and a garden where we grew the vegetables we ate. We lived among the flowers and fruit trees, and our home provided the perfect shelter for our peaceful and happy way of life.

We always had a maid in the house, some pretty peasant girl who cleaned the rooms, washed and ironed the clothes, and helped my mother in her duties. A maid would stay with us for some years until my mother would find a fitting husband for her because Mama wholly considered that life without marriage is incomplete.

When one maid married, my mother would immediately look for another peasant girl to enter our service. We all treated our maids very well and came to be very fond of them. I remember that my sister and I liked to eat the carrots and leftovers from the chicken broth from the same bowl as the maid did.

Adventures with René

My bench companion in primary school and my dearest friend was René, a girl of my own age; short in stature, chubby, with dark brown hair and a very sweet nature which she has kept all her life. At the time I am writing this, René lives in Budapest and works in the offices of the university, where she is married to an outstanding university professor. Our friendship has lasted for all these years.

René belonged to a rich Jewish farming family that owned large tracts of land on the outskirts of the village where they cultivated grapevines. Every year, a harvest festival was held in the vineyards. We often spent our vacations there, where we had wonderful times.

At school, René and I were the smallest pupils in the class, and therefore occupied the front-row bench. When we were not in school, we sometimes rode a bicycle together into the country and the neighboring hamlets where our servant girls came from.

We had a friend, Irene, whose family did not observe the rules of kosher food. They were not religious and ate bacon, pork, and some large, highly spiced sausages that gave off some exciting odors. On one occasion René and I visited the cellar of Irene's house where they kept sausages, salami, bacon, hams, and smoked legs of pork. Our Jewish faith forbade the eating of pork. But our longing was very great, and one day we went to Irene's house and asked her to give us a little of those tempting sausages. René and I shared a small piece of sausage and found it very good. But we were afraid to swallow it and spat it out. That little bit of forbidden meat made us feel terribly guilty.

Patriotism and History Lessons

On March 15, all Hungary celebrates national independence day. In Szécsény the schoolchildren paraded with the country's red, white, and green flag with the Hungarian crown in the center. It was customary for the boy or girl who had been most outstanding that year in school to carry the flag.

One year my sister was chosen to carry the flag, which filled all my family with pride.

We stood with the crowd from our town and heard the voice of the master of ceremonies call out: "And now, the best student of this year, Magdalena Davidovich, will render homage with her verse to the national flag."

My sister was small and could hardly support the banner. With an effort, she mounted the platform installed for the celebration at the foot of the monument to independence. Once there, she delivered the flag to a soldier who held it with the pole inclined. She then took the flag by a corner, kissed it, and began to recite a patriotic poem with her arms raised high.

My father was seated in the front row, beside the highest local authorities. Behind him and on the sides of the square were all the people of the village. Magdalena's performance was very beautiful and moving, and she and my parents received many effusive congratulations.

The Jewish primary school was not far from our home. To get to school, we simply crossed the patio where Mama raised her geese and hens and opened a door from the patio into the school. We never had to go out in the street. And at break, we traveled to our house for lunch in a jiffy, or my mother brought us lunch by the same delivery route.

The class I most enjoyed was arithmetic. I was very good at this subject and later at algebra.

I loved history classes with all my soul until I was eleven years old, when I began to hate it because I thought the teacher was telling us barefaced lies when he described certain events and told us that there were different races of people who had different colored skin. I also thought, maybe not without reason, that it was absurd and useless to make us memorize an unending string of names and historical dates.

I suppose my innocence about different races was somewhat admirable, but I was so sure that the teacher was pulling our leg that I refused to study, believing I would pass because the teacher was a friend of my father. Until one day the teacher sent for my father and told him, "I am going to have to fail your daughter because she doesn't know, and doesn't want to know, anything about history."

My father talked to me and explained that there actually were different races, although I didn't really believe him. But he—kindly—forced me to study history at home until I obtained the minimum marks needed to pass this subject.

A Splendid Universe

Those years remain in my memory as a time when all was new and marvelous to my innocent eyes. I was a village child, and my simple and happy life was nourished by the love of my family and the splendor of the land and nature around me. The houses and streets of Szécsény bloomed with trees, flowers, and gardens.

My small but satisfactory universe was confined to my village, its outskirts, and the Hungarian cities I occasionally visited with my parents. In all honesty, I liked Szécsény, my lovely, beloved, and pleasant birthplace, much more than the cities of Hungary.

One of these cities was Budapest, which, according to what my elders said, was considered at that time to rival Paris in elegance, culture, distinction, architectural beauty, works of art, great stores, and theater and opera performances.

A brother of my mother lived in Budapest. He had been decorated by the Hungarian government as one of the best manufacturers of German silver pieces in the country. German silver is a very resistant alloy of copper, zinc, and nickel, which is used for making lovely and distinguished objects such as coffee pots, trays, and samovars. My uncle was a highly distinguished veteran of the First World War. Because of his veteran status and his manufacturing status, he was later protected by the Hungarian government and not deported or taken to the concentration camps.

Hungary is a predominantly Catholic country, with Protestant and Jewish minorities. Hungarians are known for their deeply rooted and profound faith, and I believe that people are even more religious in the small villages like Szécsény. That may be because there are few entertainments (in my village there was only one movie theater) and also because closeness to nature seems to stimulate the religious sense inherent to human beings.

Although antisemitism has always existed in Europe, in my village the followers of the different religions lived together in harmony. The Catholic priest, the Protestant pastor, the rabbi, and the singer of the synagogue—my father—respected one another and maintained good relations. The Protestant pastor, his wife, and their six children frequently dined at our home, and we also went on occasion to eat at their home. During the village festivities, the ministers of all the religions sat in the front row next to the village authorities.

Our secondary school was not Jewish, and a Catholic priest taught the catechism. I remember that when he came to give this class, he told us, "The children who are not Catholic may withdraw if they wish, but if they want to they can stay." All the Jewish girls stayed in the class—not because we were interested in the catechism—but because the Catholic priest was very handsome!

A Consecrated Day

The most important Jewish religious celebration is Yom Kippur, the Day of Atonement, which is celebrated eight days after the Jewish New Year. The celebration is marked by prayers and absolute fasting, which begins on the previous evening. The day is consecrated to God for forgiveness of the sins committed during the year.

The following day prayers begin at an early hour and finish at night. At Yom Kippur, all the Jewish community of the village came to the synagogue, where my father stayed all the time. At nightfall, my father played the *shofar (ram's horn) as a signal of freedom from sin and reconciliation with God, thus finishing the celebration.*

In the synagogue itself, those attending then used to have a glass of schnapps (a strong pear wine used by the Hungarian peasants) and a small cake, in order to break the fasting. Then we all went back to our homes for a light supper that would not fall heavy on the stomach. I remember that my father would have a cup of tea and a plate of soup with a few noodles and a small piece of roast chicken.

During the Sabbath, the seventh day of the week, we Jews refrained from all work and dedicated ourselves to divine worship. The Sabbath is counted from sunset on Friday until sunset on Saturday. In my home, every Friday evening, after the Sabbath supper, all the family sang with my father, intoning Jewish religious chants and popular Hungarian songs. Then we went out to the street for a walk. Incidentally, my father was accustomed to go for a walk every evening after supper. When I was small I didn't understand the words of the Hebrew religious chants, but I repeated them with enthusiasm. The maid learned our songs and would sing them later in the kitchen while washing the dishes.

Trusting, Safe, Tolerant

Szécsény was such a trusting and safe village that there were no locks on our doors, and shop owners sometimes left their stores open without guard while they went to inner rooms. Customers had to shout in order to be served in the shop.

We placed bars on our doors only when traveling groups of Romani peoples—who we then called Gypsies—came to our village. These travelers were charming and picturesque but had bad reputations as being thieves. We children were afraid of them because it was said they used to steal children. But these people, although often clothed in rags, were certainly enchanting, with an elegant presence and beautiful women. And how they played the violin! (The Romani people also became targets of the Nazis and many were persecuted and exterminated like the Jewish people were.)

In the Szécsény of my childhood, no malevolence or social discrimination existed. Everyone accepted everyone else. For example, no one bothered or scolded the village prostitute, a lovely Hungarian woman with a short, tight skirt and painted face and nails. She used to walk in the middle of the street to show herself off better, trusting in the fact that there were few cars around. Old and young looked at her with the acceptance and respect which every human being deserves.

So passed my childhood, amidst songs and joy, in the warmth of the affection of family and in the happy space of a friendly and peaceful village that seemed like a large family. The Nazi barbarism had not yet arrived to poison spirits with hatred, animosity, and destruction.

CLOUDS OF HATE, STORMS OF BRUTALITY

ℐ~𝒶

UNFORTUNATELY, THIS HAPPY AND CIVILIZED way of life gradually deteriorated until it culminated in the bitter time of humiliation, suffering, and injustice for the Jews of my village and of all Hungary.

The government of Admiral Nicholas Horthy, against the wishes of the Hungarian people, allied itself to Nazi Germany. And when Hitler's forces invaded the Soviet Union, the Hungarian Army joined them, in the same way that a flea can join in the battle of an elephant. After this military alliance, the Germans gained more influence in Hungary's everyday political life and governmental decisions.

Under the Nazi influence, the antisemitism which had always existed in Europe flared up ferociously. I knew nothing of anti-Jewish sentiments until I entered secondary school. As I mentioned earlier, it was obligatory at that time in Hungary to learn German, and the pupils of the Jewish primary school learned the language conscientiously and were more accomplished in German than our fellow students in secondary school who had gone to a different primary school.

Our achievement in German was reason enough to awaken the resentment and envy of other students, and they insulted us all the time, calling out "Stinking Jews!" and spitting on the floor when we passed by.

It was very painful for me to unexpectedly discover that my religion was a target of hatred and derision. I, like my parents, brothers, and sister, loved Hungary deeply, and it was incomprehensibly cruel that children and young people who were my countrymen and fellow students would throw my Jewish status in my face as though it were a disgrace and a dishonor.

But children never invented hatred. Our fellow students were only repeating the hostile and offensive words they undoubtedly heard from their parents in the privacy of their homes. The first time that I was the object of these insults, I arrived home bathed in tears, wounded to the core. But from the lips of my father and my mother, who certainly had long known of the manifestations of antisemitism, I heard only words of peace and recommendations for tolerance and patience.

I attended secondary school for less than a year—not because of the insults thrown at me—but because the problems brought about by antisemitism multiplied until they shattered our family and community life.

To Torture and Destroy

The era of defamation and maltreatment arrived in full force one day in 1942 when I found out after arriving at school that the police had arrested my father on higher orders. He was accused of having a short-wave radio inside the piano in order to monitor the news coming from England and the United States. The accusation could not have been more absurd because we had neither radio nor piano in our house.

I can see now that my father's arrest was intended to unbalance the Jewish community by attacking the cultural and religious values represented by people such as my father, singer of the synagogue, teacher of Hebrew history, and a man who studied Jewish culture and religion.

My father's arrest cast a heavy shadow over our life at our home. We sorely missed the father who was all goodness and affection and keenly felt the absence of his wisdom, his goodness, and his protective presence. My poor mother went to Budapest each month, to the Ministry of the Interior, from functionary to functionary, to plead her husband's case, showing them irrefutable evidence of his honesty, his rectitude, and his innocence.

At last, after eight months of negotiations, my father was set free and returned home. However, he did not return to the pleasant and happy life of yore. Rather, he would soon be victim of and witness to even more imperious injustices that would be committed against the Jewish community. In fact, the entire community would soon disintegrate before the infamy of the Nazis, who now controlled the situation in Hungary at will.

I did not know that the Nazis were losing the war and that Hitler's perversity and murderous insanity was his way of avenging his losses by injuring the Jews. Nazi orders spread across all the European countries they controlled: Torture and destroy the Jewish communities.

One of these antisemitic measures was carried out in my village at the beginning of 1943. The authorities announced that Jews could not be seen in the streets of Szécsény without carrying on our clothes, sewn over the left breast, the six-pointed yellow Star of David. We poor, pacifistic, and humiliated people did not know the order had been sent from Berlin, where the official gazette of the German government, the *Reichsgesetzblatt,* explained the iniquitous disposition in this cruel and vile manner:

> *The German soldiers have come to know the Jews during the Eastern Campaign in the most repugnant and hateful manner. It has therefore been necessary to mark them with the Star of David in order that the Germans and their allies can beware of them and harass and repudiate them.*

We were the victims of the Nazis and of the cowardly path followed by the government of Admiral Horthy who, incidentally, was later imprisoned by Hitler's barbaric allies. He who aligns himself with the Devil will end up as his victim.

We Jews could not fathom why our country had ordered such a discriminatory measure that robbed us of our dignity and made us feel marked for a nonexistent crime. We were suddenly subject to an irrational mandate which denied our rights as humans.

I remember the sad case of the village pharmacist, a poor man who had converted to Catholicism when he was a child and no longer considered himself a Jew. When he was forced to wear the Star of David on his clothes because some of his ancestors had been Jewish, he committed suicide by slashing his wrists.

The terror grew considerably after we were ordered to wear the Star of David on our clothes. Neighbors who had been friendly and respectful now insulted us in the street and made us the object of their gibes and disdain.

By that time, no one sang or laughed in my house. My parents didn't want to alarm my siblings and me, but we could sense immense sorrow and discouragement in their faces and in their looks. Even so, no one anticipated the living inferno which lay in wait for us. The actions taken against Jews, without doubt, set in motion one of the blackest chapters in the history of Nazi infamy.

First the Ghetto, Then Arrests

The next step occurred soon after we were ordered to display the Star of David. The authorities ordered that all Jews would be moved into a ghetto, a neighborhood where the Jews of the village were crowded together and separated from the rest of the population. The part of town chosen for this human pile-up was around the synagogue, which was next-door to our house. Two or three Jewish families were packed into each house of this sector.

Authorities would arrive at a Jewish home when all were likely to be there and order the family to move immediately to the ghetto taking form around the synagogue. They were allowed to take only possessions for personal use. Respectful people of peaceful habits, members of the Jewish community obediently marched where they were told, leaving behind the fruits of entire lifetimes.

The Jews locked the doors of their homes and businesses as they left, naively assuming they would return some day. The few who survived were never able to reopen these doors, simply because the looters and dismantlers of those properties did not leave even the doors standing. I suppose the first looters were the German soldiers who did not delay in occupying the village. And they were followed eventually by the Russians who arrived to chase out the Germans.

My parents received those who were ordered to live with us in what was now the Jewish ghetto with their usual hospitality. And these Jewish families, who loved and respected the singer of the synagogue, behaved toward us with great kindness. We were really like one family, united and possessed by the fear of what might happen to us. My brothers, my sister, and I moved in with my parents in their bedroom while the rest of the house was divided among three other families.

The army barracks were on the same street as our house, two blocks away. Because Profeta Street was paved, the sound of the soldiers' boots and the hooves of their horses always alerted us to troops arriving at or leaving the barracks. The children of the house used to run to the window to admire the martial steps of the soldiers as well as their uniforms, horses, and weapons.

We Jewish children had never thought of the soldiers as our enemies. On the contrary, we had joined with them in the patriotic festivities. But one day not long after the ghetto had been installed in our part of town, the resonance of the soldiers' boots along the street became a sign of danger not excitement. On that day, the troops arrived at the ghetto to arrest young and adult men of the Jewish community, leaving only the old men, the sick, the women, and the children. My two brothers were in the flower of youth, and my father was a healthy man, so the three of them were arrested.

Full of anguish, my mother, my sister, and I asked them why they were arresting Papa and my brothers. They told us they were going to take them to war. That answer was impossible to believe because we knew perfectly well that civilians marked with the Star of David were never sent to the front.

Desperation mixed with panic seemed to come at us from all sides until it enveloped all three of us, feeding on our horror and our uncertainty.

In the morning hours eight days later, we heard the resonant step of the soldiers who were leaving the barracks and ran to the window with our hearts full of black foreboding. There we were struck by the terrifying reality that they were taking away our loved ones to an unknown destination. Crazed with desperation, we looked for my father and my brothers among the multitude of men who were advancing in files of five, guarded by the soldiers.

We finally managed to spot them and called their names, but they had been firmly forbidden by the soldiers to turn their heads and talk to us. My mother, my sister, and I saw the tears running down their cheeks as they advanced toward an exodus to an unknown destination, treated worse than criminals. We three women felt completely abandoned and embraced one another, weeping.

German troops entered the village in May 1944. But the old people, the sick, and the women and children who remained in the Jewish ghetto had no way of knowing whether this was good or bad for us. Some might have believed that, because Hungary was militarily allied with Germany, the Germans would feel obliged to protect us since we held Hungarian nationality. We were completely unaware of the terrifying situation happening across Europe and did not know that the German soldiers had been fully degraded by Hitler's doctrines of hatred and extermination. We had no way of knowing that they had dedicated themselves to abusing, torturing, and assassinating a considerable part of the European population. We did not know anything about this or about the cruel fate that awaited us.

Awakened To a Living Nightmare

But the Nazi evil did not delay long before putting in an appearance in all its arrogant brutality. The day after the German troops arrived, the Hungarian police, I assume on the orders of the Nazis, forced open the door of our home and broke into our bedroom. They pointed their guns at us and ordered us to abandon the house in thirty minutes and await orders in the street. We were told we could carry only one suitcase and warned not to shut the street door. They would take care of that task, they said.

We couldn't believe what was happening to us. I felt as though I was floating in the mist of an absurd dream. We felt paralyzed. However, making a superhuman effort, my mother, my sister, and I dressed like automatons and went out into the street without packing a thing. There the SS, Hitler's terrible security guards, appeared, pushing us with the butts of their weapons, shouting for us to hurry up and forcing us to walk toward the main street and then the village square with its monument to independence.

All those Nazis were very young, and they all acted with great roughness. Panic swept throughout out community, and the children wept in desperation. Shouting and threatening, the Germans ordered us to stop the children from crying. But who is able to quiet children when they are crying from anxiety and fear?

So, to the sounds of weeping children and shouts of the SS, we kept walking. What was happening to us was so incredible and so unjustified that I kept feeling that I surely must be trapped in a nightmare. Even as I write this, so many years after that infamous night, I feel for a moment that none of it ever happened. Unfortunately, it was all real, terrifyingly real.

We left Profeta Street. After the war, the name was changed to the Street of the Martyrs, in memory of so many innocent people who left that street en route to being martyred by the Nazis.

We stayed in the main street for several hours, near the little square which was already occupied by other Jewish prisoners. We did not know what was going to happen to us, but we were sure it was going to be horrifying.

Suddenly they ordered us to walk—this pathetic caravan of anguished and fearful beings—toward the outskirts of the village. My mother, my sister, and I marched very close together among the sick, children, and women until we reached an enormous stable without a roof that had been turned into a type of prison. We slept there on the ground for two or three nights, and the number of German soldiers increased by the hour. No one bothered to tell us where we were being taken. If any of us dared to ask a question of a German soldier, the latter replied with grunts and insults.

We Were the Cattle

Days later they took us to a railway station where we could see wagons used to transport cattle. Each wagon had two small barred windows no more than thirty centimeters on each side. Soon after our arrival, the soldiers opened the doors of the wagons and placed some ramps like those used to load cattle. But no animals could be seen anywhere. We were the cattle to be loaded.

However, cattle transported by train are allowed a small space to move and to lie down. We were treated worse than cattle. With blows and shoves, the German soldiers forced us up the ramps, packing us into the rail cars so tightly that we had to remain standing, squashed in like sardines in a tin. Our tormentors didn't allow one free centimeter between one body and the next.

Before pushing us into the wagons, the soldiers stripped away all packages and suitcases—the thirty kilos of luggage we had been told we were each allowed—because it would not have been possible to load so many of us into the freight wagons if any of us carried luggage. In addition, they took all personal objects such as rings, wedding rings, earrings, charms, brooches, medals—and anything else of value.

When the wagon was filled to bursting, the soldiers closed the door and fastened them with chains and padlocks. At first we could see nothing. But the little windows allowed some narrow rays of light to pass through, and after a few minutes our eyes adjusted enough so that we could perceive what a sorrowful mass of humanity we were, packed in without mercy, one on top of the other.

Many hours passed before the trains got under way. The packed car, the lack of space, the unbearable heat, the lack of oxygen, and the foul smell gave rise to a desperation which took the form of screams and weeping. Voices called out:

"Air, air, I am suffocating!"

"For pity's sake, I need space, they are pulling me apart!"

"Do not squeeze me anymore, please!"

Some of the captives fainted, while others prayed or wept from hunger and thirst.

Through the walls and the small windows of the wagon, we could hear the barking of the German shepherd dogs, trained by the Nazis for attack and a ferocity that matched that of their owners. We heard them screaming orders in German: *"Achtung!"* ("Attention!") or *"Schnell, schnell!"* ("Fast, fast!")

Fortunately, my mother was a woman of great moral strength, and in those difficult moments had the courage to transmit her exceptional serenity to my sister and to myself.

At last, when night had fallen, the train began to move. I remember the convoy often stopped, and voices, orders, and noises indicated clearly that more cars were being attached to the train, and that each one of them was packed to overflowing with unhappy human beings. So often were the stops and the cruel maneuvers repeated that I thought for a moment: "My God, they are bringing together all the Jews in Hungary to take us God knows where!"

The next day, as we sweltered in the intense May heat and from the extreme crowding, the train convoy stopped and remained stationary for half a day. No one came to help us in our pitiful situation.

Where had we arrived? Were we going to go further? We did not know, just as we did not know that we were in Auschwitz, a place known today as one of the most terrifying monuments to Nazi barbarity. For a long time, we would be ignorant of how Hitler's underlings had installed a gigantic concentration and extermination camp in this part of Poland in order to assassinate an untold number of human beings.

Sent to the Right

AT LAST, THEY OPENED THE PADLOCKS and removed the chains which closed the door of our wagon and ordered us to descend by the ramps they again put in place. We came out of the evil-smelling, hot wagon with anxiety, desperate to breathe the air and see the light. But the sun's rays were too strong, and our pupils took several minutes to adjust to the light after the semi-darkness of the railcar.

When we managed to fully open our eyes, we realized we were in a railway station, as we had supposed. The tracks had brought us inside an immense place scattered with watchtowers, surrounded by high wire fences and guarded by an army of German soldiers with dogs and machine-guns. There were so many soldiers and they were so well-armed that one would almost think they were afraid of us, a poor crowd of defenseless and pacifistic Jews. It was strange that they needed all those weapons and all those dogs to guard us.

I emphasize that we didn't have the slightest idea where we were. But when I lifted my eyes, I saw an open door about five meters high that displayed the words: *Arbeit Macht Frei* (Work Makes You Free).

I pointed out the words to Mama and to my sister. "Look what it says there. They must have brought us to this place to work."

My mother looked at the words and said to me pensively: "You are just thirteen years old and your sister fourteen, I hope you can keep on studying here." What a naive and heart-wrenching thought!

Although we had already seen the high wire fences, we turned again to look at them. They attracted our attention because of their great height; we also noticed the many watchtowers. On the top of every tower, four soldiers aimed their guns downward in four directions, in sinister and threatening groups. Worried, we looked at one another and our faces expressed the same question: "Are they going to kill us from up there?" I believe this was one of the most terrifying moments of our lives.

The space surrounded by the wire fences was enormous; it was like looking out over the sea and not being able to tell where it ended. At a certain distance one could see warehouses or factory-like buildings. Later we learned those were the barracks that contained the dormitories.

Face to Face with the Angel of Death

Suddenly, the soldiers ordered us to form in single-file lines, and a German officer appeared dressed in the elegant uniform of the SS and shod with shiny black boots. He was a tall man, young and good-looking, who carried a kind of small baton of authority in his right hand.

As we lined up, I realized the men had been separated from the women and children and taken somewhere else. Immediately, the dashing German officer, facing the line, began directing prisoners to the right or to the left with a simple gesture of his baton hand. What criteria was he using to make this division? I soon realized the children and the weak or sick-looking women were sent to the left, while the strong and healthy women were sent to the right.

My mother was anguished by the thought that, given my youth, I would be sent to the left and be separated from her and from my sister, who looked a little older. So she immediately devised a strategy. She told my sister to stand in front of me and she stood behind, whispering in my ear: "Stretch yourself as much as you can and hold your head high so that you look older, and don't separate yourself from us." I did as she advised.

When we arrived before the Nazi officer we saw that he took small children away from their strong-looking mothers to send them to the left, while the mothers went to the right. Other mothers who looked ill or weak were sent to the left along with their children.

Finally, my sister Magdalena arrived in front of the elegant Nazi officer, who ordered her to go to the right. Then it was my turn.

After we were tattooed, we were counted again, and five hundred women were taken to one of the barracks. Although the building had windows, the bunk beds that filled the space reduced the light and made it impossible to see to the end of the room.

I was given the top part of a bunk, so high it almost struck the roof of the dormitory. I had to duck my head to keep from hitting it on the ceiling in order to get into this uncomfortable place. The bunks were made of wood and included no mattress or pillow.

Night was falling when we were called for our meager supper. We were each given a tin plate with a coffee-colored stain across the bottom and a spoon that was also made of tin. We were warned that we were responsible for our plate and spoon and if we lost them or allowed them to be stolen, we would be left without food. From that night onward, we looked after the plate and the spoon as though they were treasures.

A fat woman stood outside behind an enormous cauldron. One by one we went up to her, and she used a soup spoon to place half a slice of black bread into our hands. We also were given a dark liquid that was supposed to be coffee but was actually hot, dirty water that was very unpleasant to drink. But Mama reminded us that we should consume whatever liquids and food they gave us if we wanted to survive.

After the miserable supper, we were divided into groups of five prisoners in order to facilitate counting. From then on, we stood twice a day, in the morning and in the evening, for an hour or more until one of the SS came to carry out the counting.

When we were returned to the barracks, it was not easy to get comfortable on the hard board of the bunk. We had no sheets, pillow, mattress, or blanket. The only thing we had to cover us was our dress, which we kept on when we went to bed. But it has been said that necessity is the mother of invention, and later we were able to make some thin mattresses from the straw we picked up from the floor of the dormitory, which was damp earth with some scattered wisps of straw.

I do not remember whether we slept or not on this first night in the dormitory. But I do remember we were ordered to get up at four the next morning. I thought we were getting up so early so they could put us to work, but it was actually just to place us in lines and make us stand up outdoors for the space of two hours because we were not counted until six. This two-hour wait shows that our tormentors used even the most simple requirement as a punishment.

Breakfast was the same as supper: a little repulsive liquid fancifully called coffee and half a slice of rye bread. Lunch consisted of a ration of pearl barley boiled in water. It had an unpleasant appearance, a whitish color, and an insufferable smell. Many years after my liberation, the vestiges of that disagreeable odor remained in my nostrils. It was a long time before I could free myself from that sensation and taste pearl barley without disgust.

THE HORRIBLE TRUTH
BECOMES CLEAR

WE DID NO WORK IN AUSCHWITZ. Some job would have occupied our minds, allowing us to forget a little the anguish in which we lived. I believe that the Nazis were attempting to keep us in perpetual distress and to unbalance our minds by allowing no activity.

My mother, however, was always encouraging and always confident that we would soon regain our liberty. Her company and her words were very valuable for my sister and me. Night after night we heard her pray, asking God to have mercy on us. Not once did her spirit or faith falter.

The opposite happened to me. I completely lost my faith. I no longer believed in anything except that we had been condemned to a slow death simply for belonging to the Jewish faith. I asked myself: "How is it possible that God exists and yet allows such horrible things to happen to us?"

Two days after we arrived at the concentration camp, my tattoo became infected. From the beginning, I had felt burning at the place on my left arm where they had tattooed me, but I didn't imagine that the number 2 of the identification was going to fill up with pus. I was terrified of the German soldiers, always armed to the teeth and with their ferocious dogs and didn't dare to tell any of them what had happened. Not knowing what else to do, I told the fat woman who gave us the coffee about my arm. She promised to notify the guards so they would cure me.

I supposed that they would take care of my wound in correct medical fashion, but I was wrong. Instead, they stuck the electric needle in my left forearm and superimposed a tattooed line in the infected number, drawing another 2 on top, so that the tattoo of my identification remained thus: A-20102. The number which had been erased continued to fill with pus, and it was many days before it healed. I still have the mark of the double tattoo.

As I have already noted, the railroad tracks came inside the walls of the concentration camp. About a month after our arrival, our guards ordered us to into the wagons of a convoy; our destination was known only to the Nazis. The train left Auschwitz amidst the barking of the German shepherd dogs and the shouts of the SS. Their cries of "Achtung!" and the "Heil Hitler!" salutes they exchanged among themselves made our ears ache.

Electric Fences, Gas Chambers, Crematoriums

Several Polish häftling who had been at Auschwitz for several years traveled with us. Through one of the small windows of the packed wagon, one of them showed us the wire fences surrounding the concentration camp, and they looked even higher and more imposing from our vantage point in the railcar. The Poles explained that the fences were double and that the one facing the inside of Auschwitz was electrified by a high tension current, while the outside one was normal and could be touched without danger. It was evident that the Germans had everything planned so that none of their victims could escape and avoid their horrifying fate.

The Poles said the Germans were surely taking us to work in another concentration camp, and they thought it was lucky that we were leaving Auschwitz. This place was too dangerous, they told us, because of the gas chambers and crematoriums dedicated to the extermination of prisoners.

Their words froze our blood. At that moment, my mother, my sister, and I suddenly understood why, at night, we would hear screams of anguish and pain. And we also suddenly understood the reason for the constant smell of burning flesh in that wicked camp. In our previous existence, we could never have fathomed that we would one day live in a place that included chambers and crematoriums where thousands and thousands of people were massacred!

The Polish prisoners also told us that the women and children who had been sent to the left on the day of our arrival by the elegant Nazi officer—the one they identified as the infamous and insatiable murderer Josef Mengele—had been immediately assassinated in the gas chamber. On hearing that atrocity, tears filled my eyes, because I remembered my cousin and her five-year-old son. I had just learned that they had been unjustly and brutally murdered!

The revelations made to us by the Polish women were terrifying. At Auschwitz, the Nazis' main job was to annihilate men, women, and children with absolute inhumanity.

The larger the number of prisoners rounded up by the Nazis, the faster the extermination chambers had to work. Perversely, the executioners told their victims that the gas chamber was really a bathroom and that they were being sent to shower. But the chambers were connected to deadly gas supplies by metal tubes, and when the taps were opened, gas instead of water poured from what looked like shower heads. Some of the condemned understood what was happening and hanged themselves with belts around the tubes of the sinister shower outlets.

What most entertained the bestial assassins was to let only a little gas into the chambers, so that the unhappy souls imprisoned therein did not die too quickly. They enjoyed giving them time to suffer. The pitiless executioners enjoyed hearing the screams and crying of their victims. Because the chambers had peepholes, the guards could entertain themselves by watching the anguished contortions of the dying. The macabre spectacle might last three, five, ten minutes, or longer.

Then, silence.

The bodies were then stripped of their clothing and useful elements such as gold teeth and hair before they were taken to the crematoriums with chimneys that bellowed black, thick, and evil-smelling smoke.

A Pilgrimage to Dachau, Twenty-Five Years Later

Twenty-five long years passed before I had the opportunity to see the horror of the gas chambers and the crematoriums with my own eyes. I visited the place where Hitler's henchmen mercilessly exterminated innumerable human beings during a trip I made to Austria as a tourist. I knew that Dachau was located in the south of Germany, in Bavaria. There the Nazis had installed one of their largest concentration camps where they assassinated countless prisoners, most of them Jews and Poles.

One Sunday morning during that trip, I found myself in Wiesbaden located near the Rhine River, which is known throughout Europe for its spas. That day I felt an irresistible impulse to go and see the concentration camp of Dachau which had been converted into a museum testifying to the infamies and crimes of the Nazis. The death chambers and crematoriums had been preserved just as they were in the dark days of Hitler's Germany. The idea is to keep alive reminders of this barbaric era so that the conscience of the world can never again allow another occurrence of such crimes.

Dachau is quite a way away from Wiesbaden, and I took all that Sunday to get there and back. I boarded a train in Wiesbaden very early, stayed only thirty minutes in the concentration camp, and took another train back to Wiesbaden. It was already night when I returned.

That half-hour visit has remained engraved forever in my spirit, etched with hair-raising and melancholy memories. Seeing the brutal evidence of Nazi crimes and cruelties resurrected memories of the captivity that my mother, my sister, and I suffered in different concentration camps for the space of a year.

What impulse took me to Dachau? I didn't know then and I don't know now. But it was a stronger impulse than my reason, a hidden need of my spirit to go alone to that fearful place.

Without stopping in the city of Dachau, which I had no interest in exploring, I took a taxi from the train station and told the driver:

"Take me to the concentration camp." I didn't say one word more to him. I was nervous, lost in my own thoughts, my heart beating fast.

When the driver reached the concentration camp, I paid him and got out of the vehicle. In front of me was a very high dome with four columns, crowned with an enormous cross. I was suddenly filled with a depression more profound than I had ever experienced before. Getting my emotions under control, I said to myself: "Courage, Dina, and forward!"

At the entrance to the concentration camp of Dachau are two or three rooms where they sell maps, books, photographs, and guides for visitors. There I obtained a book which contained the terrifying statistics about Dachau: how many Catholic priests had been exterminated there; how many Jews; how many Romani; how many men, women, and children of different European nationalities had been murdered there by the Nazi butchers.

On a wall in the first room, I saw a gigantic map that showed the location of all the concentration camps installed in Europe by the Germans. On it, I located the different camps where I had been held prisoner.

Lost in my painful thoughts, I did not want to talk to anyone. I even thought, "If anyone speaks to me, I will pretend I don't speak German."

The photographs I saw on the walls of the rooms were hair-raising. Some of them have been reproduced by the world press. All show an indescribable horror.

I left there with my soul destroyed and wandered through some lovely and well-kept gardens with stone sculptures in memory of the women and children sacrificed there. Farther on, I found an arrow with the words: "To the gas chambers."

I felt very ill. My nerves, already on edge, seemed to scream, and a cold sweat covered my brow. But collecting my energy, I kept on in the direction indicated, in order to verify with my own tear-filled eyes how far the cruelty of Hitler and his underlings had reached.

Only someone who has lived hours, days, and months of fear and desperation in the hell of the concentration camps would be likely to experience the agony or suffer the way I did during my visit to the extermination camp of Dachau. What I felt in Dachau went further than I can describe in words because words have their limitations and my pain was unlimited in those thirty minutes, which weighed on my soul like centuries of affliction.

When I was on the train back to Wiesbaden, I looked at the book I had acquired at Dachau. On the cover was a photograph of the entrance to the camp, highlighted by the dome and cross. On the first page, I read that the Marguerite nuns celebrate Mass every Sunday in the cupola for the spirits of the Catholic priests exterminated at Dachau. The book also noted that many more priests had been sacrificed in other Nazi concentration camps.

The following pages of the book were full of illustrations and data which, in my depressed state, did me a lot of harm. Upon reaching Wiesbaden, I threw the book away. If I had known that years later I would be writing this story, I might have kept the book so I would have more information about one of the most infamous German concentration camps. It would also be helpful to have a copy of the map where I located the camps where my mother, my sister, and I had been held.

On the other hand, I believe it is good to write this book only from my own burning memories, not based on any of the many books published on the Holocaust. My words offer the valid testimony of a woman who—as a child—lived the horrors of the German concentration camps in her own flesh.

POINTLESS WORK, MINDLESS BRUTALITY

ぐ゜ゃ๐

THE TRAIN ADVANCED AND LEFT AUSCHWITZ BEHIND. Once again we were packed in worse than cattle. Once again the rhythm of the wagons over the rails told us we were traveling to an unknown destination. Once again we suffered from the crushing conditions, which threatened to suffocate us, and the uncertainty. But our fear was greater than it had been on the trip which took us to Auschwitz because now we knew of the unbelievable cruelty and barbarism of the Nazis and of the monstrous methods they used to exterminate human beings.

I was buried in very bitter thoughts, scared by the revelations from the Polish prisoners, thinking of the gas chambers, the crematoriums, and electrified wires. Lost in my fears, I didn't even notice when the convoy at last drew to a halt. I became aware only when they took off the padlocks and chains, opened the wagon door, put the familiar ramp into place, and ordered us to descend.

The panorama in front of our eyes was gray and desolate. It looked like an outcrop of rocks where a large crowd of prisoners in gray-striped uniforms were toiling under the watchful eye of a bevy of SS guards with their weapons and their inevitable dogs.

We saw rocky hills of different heights, tunnels leading into what appeared to be a stone mine, narrow paths where little wagons filled with rocks were being pushed by prisoners. Meanwhile, other prisoners using spades and picks were digging, removing and reforming piles of stones, kicking up grayish dust that clouded the atmosphere.

One could hear the shouts of the *kapos* (chiefs), the title given by the Germans to the Polish Jewish foremen who constantly goaded the prisoners: "Work faster!" "Don't go to sleep!" "Fast, fast!" These shouts intensified when the SS supervisors came closer.

Why did the kapos treat their own compatriots and other companions in captivity with such harshness? Because it was the only way they could survive. The Germans ordered them to be merciless to the prisoners in their charge. Before they had been appointed kapos by the Nazis, these men had somehow managed to stay alive for four, five, or six years. By the time they received their position, the kapos were all too aware they would be eliminated without pity if they were not ruthless with the unhappy prisoners. And the kapos wanted above all things to stay alive, dreaming about the day of their liberation. So they were prepared to pay any price: to show cruelty to the prisoners, offer abject obedience to their Nazi masters, and even make false accusations to better their positions.

All of the European concentration camps were built with the manpower of the Jews enslaved by the Nazis. These men suffered excessively. The few who survived the harsh treatment for long had been hardened to the point where they were willing to betray, denounce, and kill their own companions if that would please the Germans. They had become evil, and their hearts had turned to stone. Thus were the kapos.

We had arrived at a concentration camp on the outskirts of Kraków, a city in the south of Poland, a country that had been brutalized by the Germans after their invasion in 1939, due to its large Jewish population. In 1943, a year or so before my mother, my sister, and I arrived in Kraków, the Jewish ghetto in Warsaw had rebelled in an act of desperation. After about three weeks, the Nazis overcame the rebels and razed the ghetto. After this uprising bathed in blood, the Germans became infinitely crueler with the Polish Jews, exterminating many of them in the gas chambers and half-starving others while forcing them into excessive work that killed many of them through sheer exhaustion.

There were no gas chambers or crematoriums at the Kraków concentration camp. However, it was still a scene of frequent violent deaths as the Nazi soldiers used whips or firearms to eliminate prisoners. In fact, it was well-known that the SS guards had taken the lives of not a few prisoners by flogging in the Kraków camp. And it was equally well-known that the despicable scoundrels greatly enjoyed using helpless captives for target practice.

I watched, horrified, as a high-ranking Nazi officer entertained himself and his four- or five-year-old son by giving the boy his pistol and urging him to use it on some terrified prisoners. The prisoners ran madly from one side to the other, trying to avoid the fatal shots.

This story seems unbelievable, but it isn't to those of us who know how the Nazis in Kraków passed their time. I remember that the child was dressed identically to his father, in the small and impeccable uniform of an SS officer. Every time a bullet hit its mark, the child laughed and was rewarded by the guffaws of his father. I do not believe the child realized the shots were real; he may have thought the men fell down as a joke, just part of an entertaining game.

The minds of the Nazis were so rotten, their souls so depraved, that they didn't even respect the innocence of their own children. Instead, they brought them up to despise human life and to enjoy crime. By these vile actions, they placed themselves lower than the beasts.

Crushing Work, Crushed Spirits

At Kraków, we did work. But it was the most stupid, unproductive, and senseless work that can be imagined.

Our work area was close to the ruins of a Jewish cemetery, and we could see broken tombstones covered with dirt. Hebrew and Polish inscriptions were visible on some of the stones. We learned later that German executioners had buried alive many Jews there and then forced the victims' families to open the graves. Some fifty yards away from this tragic cemetery was a hill, the narrow road I saw on my arrival, and a plot of land full of rocks that had been taken out of the mine.

Our work consisted of carrying these rocks by hand to the top of the hill. The next day, we had to carry down the same rocks we had moved the previous day.

In Greek mythology, Sisyphus was condemned to push a rock to the top of a mountain, but when he at last placed the heavy stone on the top, the boulder would tumble down the mountainside, and Sisyphus would have to begin again the task of rolling it back up the hill. For the victims of Nazi iniquity, our work was worse than that of Sisyphus because the rocks didn't fall down the hill by themselves; instead we had to carry them down with our lacerated hands.

At the Kraków forced labor camp, I learned by my own experience that nothing so demoralizes a human as having to carry out a completely useless task which does not benefit himself or others. The refined cruelty of the Nazis was on display as they forced us to do useless work that was not suited to women while providing a very insufficient food supply.

We had been reduced to complete inactivity at Auschwitz; in Kraków, we were forced to futilely carry stones up and down a hill. The combination and the contrast of conditions at the two locations was truly brutal.

My child's body, weakened by hunger and worn out by our exhausting tasks, was forced one night to bring stones from the interior of a mine to the surface in a heavy iron wagon that I was forced to push by myself.

To make our condition worse, the next day we were forced to carry large, heavy rocks up the hill in order to bring them down again the following day. The unmovable kapos and the ferocious SS guards were there to ensure that we carried sufficiently large rocks, while in our state of starvation and exhaustion, it was natural for us to choose smaller and lighter stones.

My mother, my sister, and I always went up and down the hill together, one behind the other, among the other prisoners who were also employed in the exhausting task. One day as we climbed the hill, an SS soldier drew near to us. Although we did not dare to turn our heads around, we knew he was coming nearer because we heard the unmistakable sound of his boots. A moment later he began shouting: *"Ferfluchte juden!"* ("Graceless Jewesses!") "The stones you are carrying are not stones, they are marbles!"

Before the soldier finished his string of insults, I felt on my back the searing and cutting blow of a whip. Afraid of being hit again or of being punished in some atrocious and unknown fashion, I did not cry or protest, even though the intense pain knocked me and my load of stones to the ground. I got up as quickly as I could, picked up the stones that had fallen, and kept on climbing. After walking a little, the pain receded, but my back felt wet and my dress stuck painfully to my skin.

My poor mother, who had seen everything, suffered indescribably as she saw my blow from a Nazi soldier who did not care about my evident weakness or small size. Mothers will be able to relate to the pain she suffered as she watched helplessly while her thirteen-year-old daughter was wounded by the whip. On this occasion, even though she was a good, resigned, and tolerant woman, my mother could not contain herself and damned the soulless Nazi who had hit me in a low voice full of anger.

The damp sensation on my back was blood drawn from the whip of the SS. When at last he moved away, between the intervention of various prisoners and with the authorization of the kapos, I was taken to the infirmary, where they treated my wound as quickly as possible and then ordered me to return immediately to the exhausting work on the hill. I was forced to carry stones once again even as I felt a searing furrow which burnt my back. The wound caused by the Nazi's whip took two months to heal. By good fortune, not even a scar remained.

Dreaming of Ending It All

After that brutal whipping, I completely lost my desire to live. What sense did it make to stay alive just to experience hunger and fear and to suffer from the most painful and barbaric punishments? What purpose was there in living in order to carry out animal-like work which was, moreover, completely useless and degrading?

Utterly exhausted and completely wretched, I remembered as in a fog the happy life I had led not long before in Szécsény. Sometimes I thought that life had been only a dream or that it had happened to some other person with my same name but who was completely separate from me.

Other girls of my age were singing, playing, and laughing. They were wearing lovely clothes and being spoiled by their elders. I was leading a miserable existence full of fear, anxiety, and troubles.

On many occasions, I gazed at the electricity-charged fences, thinking about embracing them and thus ending my life once and for all before the Nazis killed us slowly or in some sudden and pitiless fashion which they had assuredly reserved for us. After all, I would not be the first concentration camp prisoner to end her life stuck to the high-tension wires. Not a few women had done so at Kraków, despairing of their tragic lives and without hope of any kind.

I am sure I would have committed suicide without thinking much about it if it had not been for the words of comfort and encouragement from my mother and my sister. My *anyuka* (which is the Hungarian word for mother) was a woman without much schooling but infinite wisdom and an extraordinary philosophy of life. She always knew how to find the most effective words to give us strength and to make me believe we would soon be freed. Along with her love, she passed to me something of her spirit, protecting me with her wonderful faith.

But despite my mother's faith and encouragement, we continued to be treated like human rags. We had only one set of clothes—the garments we had been given the day we arrived at Auschwitz—and you can imagine how filthy and tattered they were by now. There is nothing more demoralizing for a woman than to have only one filthy and worn-out dress. There were very few bathrooms in the Kraków camp; we were rarely allowed to bathe and given no water or soap to wash our dresses or ourselves. Living in the dirt and stench of our own body odors and the odors of our companions was extremely unpleasant. Not a few prisoners died due to lack of hygiene.

I was a poor little girl terrified at every glimpse of a kapo or a Nazi, wearing my only dress, which was soiled with earth and my own dried blood that had been shed at the lash of the whip.

Some companions told us we had been in that concentration camp for two months. They had calculated the time when they heard the kapos mention dates. But it seemed absurd to me to bother to calculate dates, which could only be of interest to prisoners who knew the length of their sentence and could calculate it diminishing day by day. For us, time ceased to have any meaning, as we didn't know how long our yoke would last. We lived badly on Mondays, on Tuesdays, on Wednesdays, on Thursdays, on Fridays, on Saturdays, and on Sundays. What is the difference between one date and another when every day you carry out the same degrading work and suffer from the same hunger and humiliations?

Undoubtedly, the purpose of our Nazi jailers was to destroy us. To reach their goal, they employed the maddening work, the almost nonexistent food, the constant fear, and the misery of the completely unhappy life which they imposed on us.

My sister, Magdalena (left) was seven and I was six years old in this picture.

Magdalena (left), my brother Ernest, and I pose with my maternal grandmother before the war. Ernest was the oldest child in my family.

My mother, sister, and I were forced
to walk up ramps like this one
into the railcars that carried us to
Auschwitz. The ramps and the cars
were built to transport cattle. This
picture shows Jews being loaded into
a train in Warsaw. (This image, taken
from Wikimedia Commons, is in the
public domain, and its creator has
not been identified.)

*Like in this photo from Poland, the railcars that transported us to Auschwitz and
other concentration camps had only small windows to provide light and air. (This
image, taken from Wikimedia Commons, is in the public domain, and its creator has
not been identified.)*

After arriving in Auschwitz, we were lined up on this platform where the villainous Josef Mengele chose whether we would be sent directly to the gas chambers or to live in the torment of the Nazi concentration camps. This picture shows Jews from Hungary who had been sent to Auschwitz in late May 1944, around the time we arrived there. (This image, taken from Wikimedia Commons, is from the United States Holocaust Memorial Museum. It is part of the collection known as the Auschwitz Album and was donated by Lili Jacob, a survivor, who found it in the Mittelbau-Dora concentration camp in 1945.)

After murdering hundreds of people at a time in the gas chambers of Auschwitz, the Nazis sent the victims' bodies to a crematorium like this one, where they would be burned in these giant ovens. Although I never saw the crematorium, the odor of burning flesh constantly hung over the camp. This photo was taken by U.S. Army Pfc. W. Chichersky at the Buchenwald concentration near Weimar, Germany, in April 1945. (This image, taken from Wikimedia Commons, is included in the U.S. National Archives and Records Administration.)

We arrived in Mexico City in May 1947. This photo was taken two months later, when I was 16 years old.

I obtained this International Red Cross ID while we were living in Paris. This documentation helped us get the support we needed in Paris and the chance to travel to Mexico.

A Brief Glimpse of Humanity

I AWOKE ONE NIGHT WITH AN EXCRUCIATING PAIN that hit me in the left armpit like a knife. My suffering was so great that I could not lower my arm. I touched my armpit with the fingers of my right hand and discovered a lump as big as an orange. When I touched it, the searing pain made me cry out and begin to weep.

My mother came quickly and climbed to my bed but couldn't see me in the total darkness. However, she touched me and realized I had a high fever and was shivering. I took her hand and placed it on the swelling under my arm. She grew very scared and said, "It's a tumor full of pus."

Perhaps the tumor formed in my armpit due to some movement or a blow that injured me and then became infected. Or perhaps it was the lack of protein and minerals in our diet, aggravated by the filth and lack of hygiene we were forced to live in. Only God knows. But the swelling had come on suddenly as I had felt nothing before I woke in the night.

Among the many prisoners in our dormitory were some Polish women who had worked in the concentration camp kitchen for several years, including the woman who distributed our rations at breakfast, lunch, and supper. She was a long-suffering woman with rather rough ways, but she had a good heart. My mother woke the Polish woman, who asked sleepily, "What do you want?"

Mother told her about my condition, and the Polish woman roused herself and promised to help. But she warned, "We can do nothing until they count us at dawn, you know what discipline is like here; and you must see what you can do so that your daughter is there standing up. Don't worry, it will soon be four. Once the counting is over, we will take your daughter to the infirmary so that they can look after her."

My mother came back to my bunk to console me and to tell me that it would soon be light and that they were going to cure me that very day, explaining, however, that I had to be present when the prisoners were counted. She told me I shouldn't worry because she would make sure that everything would be all right. Trying to instill confidence in me with her sweet and loving words, she remained by my side until the dawn.

When it was time, my mother and sister lifted me down from the bunk in their arms, and we walked together out of the dormitory to the place where we lined up. It was essential for the count to be correct that morning; if there were any problems, it would be more difficult to find a chance to take me to the infirmary. Whenever a prisoner was not in her place in the line, the Nazis would become angry and sound the alarm. Then the camp would be placed in alert, while the guards ran around everywhere, ready to gun down the missing woman when they found her.

I felt extremely weak and was sure I was going to die there and then. I tried to stand up, but felt myself fainting. My mother and sister lay me down on the grass until the moment of the count arrived. Then, with infinite care and tenderness, Mama and Magdalena quickly lifted me up when the SS appeared, so the guard could see our file of five prisoners was complete.

My sister lined up as usual in front of me, while my mother placed herself behind, holding me so I wouldn't fall to the ground and whispering words of loving encouragement. But I was extremely weak. The pain of my armpit was unbearable, my body was perspiring profusely, and my legs refused to hold me up. As I was held by my mother, my vision and mind clouded over. I felt myself falling into a deep abyss, and I knew no more.

Surprising Treatment

When I came to my senses, I found myself on a bed in the infirmary, and I heard a woman's voice saying: "This tumor must be opened at once because it is highly infected." Another female voice said: "The girl has too high a fever, and the fever will not fall unless we operate as soon as possible."

On hearing these words, I felt much more tranquil. I understood that these people were not going to kill me and that they were even willing to try to cure the tumor in my armpit. A moment later, three women—one covered with a white overall—lifted me in their arms and placed me onto a kind of high bed or operating table. One of the women said, "You must be calm, child, because what we are going to do to you will not hurt and in three days you will be well."

Two of the women then held me firmly, keeping my left arm high. Without giving me any anesthetic or even a sedative, the third woman took a knife and stuck it in my armpit. A searing pain extended from my armpit throughout my body, shaking me in a horrifying manner. I screamed and fainted.

When I next opened my eyes, it was nighttime. My armpit was still painful, but I began to feel a little better. I saw a lighted lamp and a nurse sitting in a chair, who heard me say, "schmerc" ("it hurts"). The nurse looked at her watch and no doubt realized it was the moment to administer a painkiller. She got up and came back with a pill. I sat up a little in bed so that I could drink it with water. Then I fell into a deep sleep which lasted until dawn.

I cannot remember if they bathed me or if they cleaned my body with a sponge or in some other way. But I remember that I was naked and covered with a clean, white sheet and that my body was also clean.

Truthfully, the women who looked after me in the infirmary—possibly Germans—treated me well, which makes me think that not all the souls of those running the Kraków concentration camp were rotten and full of evil.

The day after my tumor was opened, the nurses at the infirmary tried to get me to stand up, but I fainted from weakness. They placed me in bed again.

Notwithstanding the good treatment I was getting, I wanted to get out of the infirmary as quickly as possible. I was panic-stricken when I considered that they might not take me back to the dormitory and that I would never see my mother or my sister again. I wanted to be with them so much! So I asked one of the nurses to send me back to recover in the dormitory, where my mother and my sister could look after me and cure me. The woman smiled but did not reply. I could not tell if her smile was mocking my request or expressing compassion for my situation.

As I continued to be naked under the sheet which covered me, I asked one of the women for my dress and clogs. She told me, "Don't worry about them, we are going to give you some clean new ones."

Joyful Reunion

I remained in the infirmary for four days and was looked after kindly by the women there. They gave me sedatives for the pain and were never harsh or unkind to me. Their sense of responsibility and their kindness were far above the typical Nazi behavior.

After four days, the nurses sent me back to the dormitory, escorted by an SS woman. I was anxious to see my mother and sister again, but when I reached the barracks, they were out carrying stones.

I tried to take my place in my bunk, but I was still too weak to climb up to my usual place. The SS woman indicated that I should take my mother's bunk, which was below.

My mother and sister were overjoyed to find me in the barracks when they returned, and we laughed and cried and hugged each other tightly. They had been terrified that they would never see me again as they had been given no news after I was taken to the infirmary.

They weren't allowed to go near the infirmary, and no one would answer any questions about me. They didn't know if the nurses would actually care for me and were afraid I had died or been transferred to another concentration camp.

Everyone in the dormitory was delighted to see me, and hundreds of prisoners crowded around me, wanting to hear about my time in the hospital. I could tell they barely believed me when I told them the nurses had operated on me and treated me very well. So I showed them my new dress and clogs and the wound from the operation on my armpit, which was already healing.

I still have that scar. That's how I know my time in the concentration camp hospital was real. Without the scar, I might think it was all a dream.

The women in the dormitory told me it was a miracle I had returned; they had been certain they would never see me again, although they hid those thoughts from my mother and my sister. They told me the poor things had suffered greatly, thinking of me all the time and weeping bitterly all night.

Although I had returned, I was very weak and so pale that I appeared transparent. The other prisoners saw my condition and gave me special attention. I even awakened the compassion of the Polish woman in charge of distributing food, and she began giving me a little more pearl barley and a whole slice of bread at each meal instead of the regulation half-slice.

But I only got extra food for three days before someone informed the Nazis what the Polish woman was doing. It was probably one of the kapos who betrayed the woman, who was sent to work in the stone mine as punishment. The kapos were despised because of such actions, but I will never forget that humble and good woman who paid dearly for her kind gesture toward me.

We spent three months at that concentration camp located on the outskirts of Kraków, and our time there was filled with exhausting work and bitter experiences. Then one morning we were roused from our bunks and lined up outside the barracks. We didn't know what was going on but suspected some of our companions in misery had escaped so the guards needed to count us.

Instead, they put us on a train leaving Kraków.

Anguish and uncertainty grew as we rode for hours in the miserable and pestilent railcar. We were all wondering: Where are we going now? What new hell is reserved for us?

Neither More Nor Less Than Hell Itself

9⟶✧◌

IT WAS LATE AFTERNOON when the convoy stopped and we crowded to get a glimpse of our surroundings from the tiny windows. What we saw petrified us. We were back at Auschwitz!

Auschwitz! We had been returned to the accursed extermination camp, with its high electrified wire fences, its towers with four armed guards at each, its death chambers, and its infamous crematoriums!

I felt as though I were going to faint, convinced of my bitter destiny. For this had they cured me at the infirmary in Kraków? For this they had given me kind care, the new dress, the new clogs? They saved me from death in the hospital so they could send me to die in a black well of crimes and horrors?

Feeling sick, I remembered how my cousin and little nephew had been taken from us on the day when we first arrived at Auschwitz. They were sent with a crowd of unhappy souls to be exterminated in the gas chambers. Would our unmerited suffering also end in that terrifying place?

We were soon to find out during the most terrifying night of our lives. When we got down from the train we saw black smoke boiling up from a red-brick chimney about fifty meters away. We now knew that was a crematorium. Next to it were two other buildings that looked like a type of warehouse without windows. Without doubt, those were the gas chambers.

It was eight or nine at night when the brutal SS drove us like cattle into one of these sinister buildings. My teeth chattering, I said to myself: "Everything is over, they are going to kill us."

At the door of the building, the SS guards ordered us to leave our clogs and take off our dresses. Naked and shivering from cold and fright, we entered that strange, imposing place one by one. The room was dark and the floor was damp and muddy. A strong odor of chloride brought tears to our eyes and made us cough.

The SS pushed more and more prisoners into the space until we felt there was no room for even one more person. But the guards kept shouting and waving their weapons and loosing their snarling dogs as they shoved more naked women into the room, squashing us without pity in that chloride-smelling darkness. We could hear screams and heartrending weeping coming from some unknown nearby place.

It wasn't hard to understand what was happening. We were in the anteroom of a gas chamber—only a few steps away from our final torture and our extermination.

Nothing felt very important to me at this point. I saw our approaching death as the end of all our sufferings and misfortunes. Only my mother—extraordinary woman!—had the courage to tell us, "Be calm, everything is going to be all right, someone up there will save us."

A Hungarian woman who heard my mother shouted at her indignantly, "What is that? Someone up there is going to worry about us? Don't talk nonsense! Who do you think is going to prevent these animals from killing us?

"Perhaps you haven't realized where we are? Can't you hear the death shrieks a few steps away from us? Do you believe, idiot, that they are crying because they are being fed or kept amused? They are killing those people and we are the ones to follow!"

Another woman joined the shouting. "Be quiet, you! What matter if they kill us and end our martyrdom! Why the devil do you want to keep on living?"

Then another woman spoke up. "Shut up! Don't use up the oxygen! Don't you realize there is no window here and there are five hundred women who have to breathe?"

We didn't know who had just spoken, but the crowd listened to her, and a sudden silence fell, broken only by heavy breathing and soft moans. But the silence was more horrifying because it allowed us to better hear the screams coming from the gas chamber a short distance away. Some lasted quite a long time; others ended quickly. It all depended on the executioner who operated the gas keys and how much gas he sent to the chamber.

A Nightlong Nightmare

That room was neither more nor less than hell itself. Time passed painfully and slowly as we huddled there, naked and terrified, slipping on the muddy floor, feeling the air grow heavy as the oxygen was depleted but always aware of the penetrating smell of chloride.

From time to time, we heard someone in a different part of the room yell, "Don't step on me!" Or "Get up!" Or "What happened to you, woman? Where do you think you're going to sit down?" But no one ever answered these demands because the women who stopped standing were not choosing to sit down. They were dead. They had just died of fright, of hunger, of illness—or of asphyxiation.

But we did not know how many women had died in that room until the next morning, when we suddenly heard the unexpected noise of a key in the lock. The door swung open and the clear light of day poured over the room. Upon seeing the dead women around her, one prisoner wept disconsolately and screamed, "'These poor companions did not want to sit down to rest! They died in the horror and pressure of the night of hell which we have just passed!"

Six Nazis appeared. One of them shouted a lot. The prisoners who did not speak German thought that the SS shouter was angry because we were still alive. But he was actually angry we had been left in that room overnight.

He was saying, "What the devil are these women doing here? Who was the imbecile who shut them up in this place? Can't you see that they are a group of tattooed women coming from Kraków? Get them out of here at once!"

We exited that miserable, windowless building, stepping out of a nightlong nightmare that I will always relive in my bitterest moments. Most of us had been sure we would never see the sunlight again. Only my mother had held on to hope. In the most difficult moments, she was always sure that a superior power, "someone up there," would save us. When other women allowed themselves to be carried away by desperation, Mama had faith—faith which saved us from death.

As soon as we left the anteroom to the gas chamber, we were given new clogs and new dresses and ordered to form into a line to be counted. Upon finishing the count, the SS began shouting, "The headcount is not complete! There are ten women missing! They must be found at once!"

But they soon realized that ten bodies had been left behind in the anteroom of death. Ten women who died of hunger, of illness, or—most likely—of terror. After living through that night of terrible fear, I am convinced the panic was more than their anguished, weakened hearts could bear.

My Mother—the Saint

We had been a day and a half without eating anything, and our captors took us to one of the barracks where we were given the same frugal breakfast as always. But today it tasted wonderful to us because we had escaped from death and were enjoying a return to life.

That night of torment marked the most dramatic and difficult point of our affliction. After that experience, we returned to the forced inactivity of Auschwitz, where we had nothing to do. But this lack of work was a welcome respite after the exhausting work at Kraków, offering a rest much needed by our weakened and famished bodies.

However, it was excruciating to live in a place where gas chambers and crematoriums were in use. We now knew that the smell of burnt flesh we inhaled daily came from the burning of human beings exterminated by the Nazis.

As soon as we were installed in one of the barracks, two of our fellow prisoners came to my mother. These two Hungarian women apologized for having shouted at her so rudely in the anteroom of the gas chamber when she had said that God would save us. I was surprised that these women had realized it was my mother who had spoken aloud her faith, given the darkness and pressures of that horrible night. I asked how they had known the voice they had heard belonged to my mother.

They told me, "For a long time we have identified your mother as the woman who, no matter how difficult the situation, prays and trusts in God. And now, after what has happened, we believe in the power of her prayers and we bless her. Your mother, dear child, is a saint."

These women were sisters-in-law, the wives of two brothers, both doctors, from Budapest. As we continued talking, they told us they had also been with us when we arrived at Auschwitz the first time. One of them wept as she told us her children of ten, twelve, and fourteen years of age had all been sent to the left that day, that is, to the gas chambers. They were very surprised that I, who had been barely thirteen years old, had not been sent to the left but had been allowed to live. They assured me I had been allowed to live because God listened to my mother and protected her.

In this respect, I believe Mama was, without doubt, a woman of great spiritual strength; but she was also full of initiative and very brave. It should not be forgotten that she had encouraged me to appear taller and thus outwit Mengele, the "Angel of Death."

"Praying to God and striking out with the mace." That saying well describes my mother, a woman who never stopped fighting or looking for ways to get ahead.

During the long hours of enforced inactivity of our second stay at Auschwitz, we became good friends with the Hungarian women, who showed more and more affection toward my mother, my sister, and me.

Inspiring Disappearance

Not long after our initial conversation, the Hungarian women began to behave mysteriously and were often seen talking between themselves. My mother, who was an observant and wise person, realized they were planning something.

And one day, with great caution, they hinted to us that they thought they could see the possibility of "saving themselves," which is how they phrased it, instead of saying "escaping." We might have thought they were just dreaming as a way to make their captivity more bearable, contemplating an impossible act that made prison less harsh. However, these two Hungarian women turned out to be very serious.

A week later, there was something wrong with the SS morning count. The alarm sounded in the camp, and the soldiers ran about shouting, entering, exiting, and re-entering the barracks. We did not know what had happened. We stood in line for two hours and endured five counts before one of the Nazi officers came to our group of prisoners and wrathfully bellowed that two häftling were missing.

He asked us to tell him at once anything we had heard about escape plans from our companions in the barracks. Even before the SS officer spoke, Mama, my sister, and I suspected that the two sisters-in-law had escaped from Auschwitz. But afraid of reprisals, we dared not turn our heads toward the spot our friends usually stood to verify whether, in fact, they were missing.

The Nazis were extremely vengeful and arbitrary and they blamed the escape on all the prisoners who slept in the same barracks as the fugitives. They spent the day punishing us. Although we had already been standing for two hours, they made us stand for another one in the same posture. They then ordered us to kneel and then obliged us to lie on the ground face down, with our arms by our sides. They rotated these punishments throughout the morning and afternoon while giving us no food or water for the entire day.

Weak as we were, some prisoners fainted from weariness, drawing lashes from the Nazi whips. It was a very harsh punishment. But it was worth it.

We were all filled with happiness to know the two Hungarians had escaped from the concentration camp. We were glad because these two good women deserved their freedom. But we were also glad because we realized it was possible to escape from Auschwitz, despite its high electrified wire fences, its numerous watchtowers with four well-armed soldiers each, and the soldiers with their machine guns and their fierce dogs. A sweet hope was kindled in our hearts.

"So it is possible to escape from Auschwitz!" we said to each other.

However, our happiness was dulled because we did not know whether the two Hungarians had managed to avoid the Germans outside the concentration camp or if they had been arrested or murdered. During the night I heard my mother praying, asking God for the liberty of the fugitives.

How did our friends manage to escape? Only they knew, but I imagine someone from among the caretakers of Auschwitz must have helped them in order for them to have been able to escape from that closely-watched place.

On the Move Again

Around the month of September we began to notice that the Nazis were nervous and preoccupied. We knew nothing of what was going on beyond the confines of Auschwitz, so we had no way of knowing that the Allies were beginning to occupy German territory and had already freed Holland.

One day that September, we were once again loaded onto a train. Even without knowing our destination, we were happy to leave Auschwitz behind. Leaving that place, with its gas chambers and its crematoriums and the room where we had passed the most horrifying night of our lives, was healthy for the soul.

A cold autumn wind was blowing when we boarded the train, and we could not help but think that winter was coming soon. If we were not given suitable clothing, we would surely die of cold especially because our natural resistance had been depleted by hunger and bad treatment.

Once the train was in motion, the cold crept in through the walls of the wagon, making our teeth chatter. One could read the same question on every emaciated face: "Where will they take us this time?"

FACTORY "WORK" AND THE DAY OF PARDON

THIS NEW TRIP IN THE PRISONER-PACKED TRAIN lasted approximately half a morning. Minutes after the convoy stopped, the guards removed the padlocks and chains, opened the doors, and ordered us to descend.

To our surprise, we were looking at a completely different scene than the inhospitable panoramas of Auschwitz and Kraków. Because I had lived most of my life in a village filled with flowers and trees, my spirit was comforted to see trees and grass, even though the dry golden leaves of the trees were being carried away by the wind and the grass was beginning to turn yellow.

It was very cold and we were ordered to form up in lines without delay. The count was made quickly and we were immediately taken to a barracks where each of us was given a coat and a blanket to cover ourselves with at night. But our feet, naked in the wooden clogs, continued to be exposed to the cold.

We were then taken to eat and discovered the food was less bad than usual. It consisted of a thick soup of pearl barley boiled with some vegetables and meat. We were also given a slice of black bread and a teaspoon of butter.

We did not know the name of this concentration camp or the place where it was located. But we realized it must be near a village or city because we could see a road about 150 meters beyond the wire fences. Many people were traveling on the road, some of them by bicycle.

I sighed while recalling the happy days when my friend René and I mounted our bicycles and rode around the picturesque outskirts of our village. Nostalgia took over my heart as I remembered that happy life. I could see that only 150 meters away from me there were still free people, while I was a prisoner who had committed no crime other than belonging to the Jewish religion.

It was then that I thought: What if I became a bird? Then it would be easy for me to fly over the wires and go wherever I wanted. A bird who would fly freely on the wind and do only what it wanted. Oh, if only I could become that bird now!

When I woke up from my beautiful daydream, I noticed the other prisoners were also looking in the same direction, gazing at what could be seen beyond the wire, also lost in their own thoughts. At times it is necessary for the depressed spirit to dream, and I am sure that all my companions were thinking, each in her own way, of the same things I had dreamed of: liberty, that precious jewel which is only truly valued when it has been lost.

The dream of liberty, when you live in a prison, is the most lovely, sad, and wonderful of all the dreams which can be dreamed by a human being!

Our first day at this new concentration camp was peaceful. The camp was quite small and so did not have the excess of German soldiers like were in Auschwitz and Kraków. Neither were there gas chambers or crematoriums, thankfully.

Around six in the evening, when daylight began to pale in the sky, the SS quickly carried out the count because they were very cold, just like we were. And at around seven o'clock they gave us coffee for supper and a slice of bread and butter. Then they sent us to sleep.

The dormitory was damp and cold. Our blankets were rough as they were made of sackcloth. But at least they protected us a little from the cold of the night.

Sorting Parts and Making Holes

They got us up at five in the morning, counted us and gave us black coffee and a slice of bread and butter for breakfast. Afterward they told us to line up once again so they could take us to work.

Guarded by the SS, we walked around 200 meters until we reached a factory building. Four middle-age men dressed in high-quality civilian clothes waited for us outside. The SS withdrew and the men invited us to pass inside the building.

The four men, addressing us courteously, distributed us at work tables that held stamping machines. They placed my sister before one of these machines at a small table. Mama and I were placed at a large table covered with wooden boxes and nuts of different sizes.

One of the men told Mama and me, "This is a factory dedicated to making small aircraft parts. Your work consists of classifying the nuts in accordance with size and placing them in those boxes."

My sister was ordered to make holes in some metal sheets using the stamping machine. We were all allowed to sit down while doing our tasks in the factory, evidence that treatment of prisoners had been humanized to a certain extent in this place.

But it was not long before we realized that, as in Kraków, the work we were doing was useless. Instead of carrying stones up and down a hill, here we classified nuts or made holes in metal sheeting without any purpose. It seemed the only real purpose was to keep us busy with something.

It does not cease to baffle me that the Germans did not make use of a labor force that, properly channeled, could have helped them in their war effort. However, it was better for us that our work turned out to be completely unproductive because that meant our labors did not benefit the Nazis in their war effort.

Every morning when we went to work in the factory, we passed groups of women in civilian clothes such as those worn by middle- or upper-class women and girls in the cities. They were guarded by other women dressed in civilian clothes. We never knew who they were nor if they slept at the barracks or in some neighboring city. They were probably women opposed to Hitler's regime who had been taken to carry out some obligatory work. Or prisoners with certain privileges, since they were allowed to use their own clothes. They always attracted my attention and were always an enigma.

Two days after we began our work at the supposed factory for aircraft parts, my sister accidentally pierced her index finger with the stamping machine. She cried out and one of the women in civilian clothes who was in charge of the factory came running. She helped Magdalena free her hand from the machine and took her to the infirmary, where they carefully treated the wound and bandaged her hand. Then they made her return to work as soon as the treatment was over.

Pouring Out Our Pain to God

We had been at this camp for a week when, as we lay in our bunks, a prisoner said, "If I remember rightly, in these days Yom Kippur, or the Day of Pardon, is celebrated. Whether or not it is the correct date, since in these places we do not know exactly in what day we live, I invite you to celebrate this religious festival with the traditional fasting and songs. By doing that we will be nearer to God and He will pay more attention to us."

We all agreed. Although we did not dare to ask for a holiday the next day, we did ask our keepers to let us have a little more supper because we planned to fast the next day.

Luckily, they agreed. After our supper, as the last daylight disappeared and the sky became full of shadows, we withdrew to the dormitories and a woman collected all her strength to sing the Kol Nidre, the traditional prayer which commences the festival of Yom Kippur, with a strong and emotion-filled voice. I have believed since childhood that this is the most beautiful prayer of the Jewish religion, and it is the one that has most deeply touched my spirit.

The Kol Nidre, sung by the prisoner, touched our hearts that night. A great sob rose from countless throats and spread throughout the barracks. Many of us joined in the sacred chant with voices filled with infinite sadness and pain.

In my mind an image rose with absolute clarity of my father intoning the religious chants of Yom Kippur at the Szécsény synagogue. On the evening of the following day, he would sound the shofar to end the celebration. My eyes filled with tears because I didn't know where Papa was or even if he was still alive. I also thought of my brothers, remembering the nights in which my family had gathered together in blessed peace in our village house.

When the Kol Nidre ended, we sobbed and cried.

"Why, my God, why?"

"Lord, what have we done to be thus punished?"

"What sin have we committed to be treated in this way?"

"Where are those we love?"

"Pity, my God, pity!"

Thus we gave voice to our feelings until, worn out from so much weeping, we slept.

The following day we fasted. We worked the whole day without eating or drinking, consecrating our abstinence to God. Only when night fell did we eat the supper they gave us: a plate of pearl barley with vegetables and meat, a slice of black bread, and butter.

The War Draws Closer

The days, the weeks, and the months went by while we continued our monotonous and useless work at the factory. Every day it was colder, and each day we felt weaker and more demoralized, seeing only shadows in our future. Only my mother persisted with her prayers and was certain that God would come to save us.

The snow began to fall as a bitter winter arrived, and our bodies suffered greatly. We lacked defenses and were prone to fall ill at any time. It did not take long before some of us fell ill with pneumonia. The poor victims were taken to the infirmary, but we never heard any more of them. We did not know if they recovered, died of the disease, or were killed.

Toward the end of January 1945, we began to hear the constant and deafening roar of gunfire and bombing, which indicated the war was very close to us. The airplanes flew over our heads, almost at the level of the concentration camp, but we could not distinguish which country they belonged to.

We realized the Germans would soon be defeated; but, instead of making us happy, the thought filled us with fear. We were sure that they would kill us all before they withdrew or surrendered.

But they didn't.

A Trail of Blood
and Bodies

WHEN THE ALLIED TROOPS GREW CLOSE enough to force the
Germans to abandon the concentration camp, they decided to take
us with them on what came to be known as a death march. I don't
really know why.

One night around ten o'clock, they shouted at us to evacuate
the barracks as quickly as possible, and we left the concentration
camp during a heavy snowstorm. Threatening us with their weapons and their dogs, they forced us to retreat with them. But we had
no idea that this terrible walk in the snow would last for three days
and three nights.

The temperature kept falling. Wracked with cold, our clothes felt
paper-thin. As usual, my mother, my sister, and I walked together.
Although we did not know where the Germans were taking us, we
felt caught in the clutch of a doomed destiny.

As we marched under subhuman conditions, we continued to hear
the noise of gunfire and bombing in the distance. But around us was
nothing, absolutely nothing. Only abandoned land covered by snow.
A white immensity. Never during our journey did we see a city, a
town, or a village.

During those three days when we walked over a frozen inferno,
in the company of the Germans fleeing from their enemies, we were
given only one slice of bread a day. To quench our thirst, we gathered
snow in our hands and sucked it. The Nazis continued to be as cruel
and inhumane as always, immediately killing our companions who
could no longer go on because of fatigue, frozen limbs, or illness.
I will never be able to erase from my mind the tragic path we left

behind us: the dark mass of murdered corpses, the blinding whiteness of the snow, and the deep red of the blood spilled by the Nazis. The Germans decided we should rest for six hours every night. But where could we rest in an immense wilderness of snow? Where could we sleep if there was not even a small roof or a corner to shelter us? As tired as we were, the Germans ordered us to clear small spaces in the snow where we could sit and lie down. With our frozen hands, we began digging in the snow, clearing it away as well as we could and then falling exhausted on the frozen ground.

We slept at once as we had been for walking twenty-four hours without stopping. It was a miracle we managed to wake up instead of remaining frozen forever.

It was very difficult to get up. We felt our legs were paralyzed as they had become numb to the point of freezing. My mother could not reactivate her legs. When my sister and I could move, we vigorously massaged her lower extremities. We were very scared because we knew that if the Germans realized that Mama could not walk, they would kill her at once. It was quite a while before she reacted, but she was finally able to stand up and continue the march at our side. But she began to suffer from sharp pains in her knees on that march and they plagued her the rest of her life.

We renewed the march, wracked with cold, worn out, and half-dead from hunger. We were given no breakfast because the Germans no longer had food even for themselves. We moved like sleepwalkers, expecting at any minute to fall down and never rise again.

The roads were practically obliterated by the snow. Many companions fell down that day, worn out by fatigue. The Nazis killed them and left their bodies behind. Like a cavalry soldier puts a bullet in a horse with a broken leg, the Nazis finished off our companions who could no longer walk. There was no mercy.

We Belonged to the Nazis

Why did the Germans take us with them? They knew perfectly well they had lost the war and would soon be totally overthrown. Why not leave us in the concentration camp instead of forcing us to make this atrocious walk in the snow? These troops certainly had been ordered to force us on this march because Hitler's government considered concentration camp prisoners as its property, a kind of human cattle which they could dispose of as they pleased. We belonged to the Nazis so they could torture us, exterminate us, or take us wherever they wished.

Our status as property allowed them to draw us through that white and immense hell in which so many of our companions fell dead and were covered by the white shroud of the snow. But in our constant walking, the noise of the battles sounded closer than ever, showing the proximity of the armies fighting against the Germans.

That afternoon, we thought we saw something like a building in the distance but worried that it was only a mirage of our wearied minds. But as we kept advancing, that vision kept coming nearer and becoming more precise. At nightfall, we reached the place we had seen from far away.

It was an abandoned, half-destroyed concentration camp, with broken windows and missing a wall. We remained all through the night at the place we later learned was called Kratzo.

A few minutes after we arrived, a German army truck appeared carrying coffee and bread, which were distributed among us. The soldiers appeared exhausted, mere shadows who searched silently for a place to throw themselves down to sleep.

As for the prisoners, we devoured the bread and eagerly drank the hot coffee, happy to at last lie down to sleep under cover. Unfortunately, the abandoned camp of Kratzo was infested with fleas and bedbugs, and our emaciated bodies were soon covered with bites.

The German supply truck carrying coffee and bread did not depart overnight and provided us with breakfast the next morning. We then once more began to march. By the third day of walking, our group had diminished considerably, and many familiar faces were missing. Only the strongest or the most determined managed to survive the hard walk in the snow.

A Warm French Welcome

That night we arrived at another concentration camp and once again found ourselves surrounded by high wire fences, numerous Nazis with their dogs, and tall watchtowers housing well-armed soldiers. From what we could see, the place was not very large and did not contain either gas chambers or crematoriums.

By the time we arrived, we were more dead than alive, longing for a piece of bread and a corner in which to sleep.

A group of Frenchwomen received us at the camp, offering us their songs and their laughter. I imagine that when they saw us arrive almost dead from hunger, cold, and fatigue, their good hearts stirred them to shower us with their humor and affection. Their goodness and congeniality were almost irresistible, but we could only smile weakly at them. What we most needed at that point was food, a bed, and a little warmth.

Recognizing our exhaustion, the women tried to convince the Nazis to allow us to take our supper to our beds, but they did not succeed. The Nazis decreed that new arrivals who did not go out to form in line would not receive supper. Despite our hunger, not a few companions preferred to remain in the barracks to sleep because they were even more exhausted than they were hungry.

The following morning, the French prisoners—women of great character, very spirited and communicative—told us they had been at that concentration camp for three months and said they had also come from Auschwitz. We had not seen them in our times at Auschwitz because prisoners were confined in different sections of the camp based on the letters of our tattoos. Those sections were separated by high, electrified wire fences.

The Frenchwomen, who soon became our loyal friends, told us some of the terrible things they witnessed or knew had occurred at Auschwitz. They had seen the barracks where Josef Mengele, the Angel of Death, who was trained as a doctor, carried out monstrous experiments on male and female prisoners. After making them suffer horribly in his laboratories, he then sent his subjects to the gas chambers.

We told them of the horrific night we lived in the anteroom of one of Auschwitz's gas chambers and how ten of our companions died on that occasion, probably from fear.

We Could Die at Any Moment

At this concentration camp, none of the prisoners worked, except for doing some sweeping chores. Our life was very wretched, and every day we felt weaker and hungrier, and food became more and more scarce. I was sure our end was near and that we would certainly die of hunger little by little, one after the other. I also feared that one day it would occur to the Germans that they should take us to another concentration camp where we would suffer new atrocities.

I remember a solitary man, of humble condition, dressed in civilian clothes, who entered the camp every day with some vegetables for supper. He never said anything to us, only looked at us with eyes full of tremendous melancholy. Was this look of deep sadness because he saw our wretched condition as prisoners, every day more famished and emaciated? Or was it the reflection of his own misfortunes and sufferings because of the war? We never knew, but the gaze of that silent man moved me greatly, transmitting to me a whole world of nightmare and abandonment.

In this way, the days, the weeks, and the months passed by. We thought we could die at any moment—maybe from artillery fire, which sounded very close and at all hours, or from a bomb dropped by one of the planes that flew very low over us and made us lift our eyes to heaven as though to implore them to free us or to kill us once and for all. Just put an end to our nightmare.

Toward the end of March, the air was still quite cold, but the sun shone again in the heavens, offering a little warmth to our pale, anemic, almost translucent skin.

Our appearance was pitiable and pitiful by then. Our hair, which had been shaved off the first time we arrived at Auschwitz, had grown some four or five centimeters. Depending on it texture, the hair stuck to the skull of some prisoners, while it stood stiffly on end like the bristles of a brush in others. The appearance of our returning hair would have made us laugh if it had not been for our constant sadness. Moreover, our hair represented a sign of our misfortune, so our appearance did not seem funny to us.

April came, the eleventh month of our captivity. Eleven months may seem a short time for those living a normal and peaceful life. But for my mother, my sister, and I, those months had delivered a lifetime of suffering, humiliation, hunger, and fear. The months weighed on us like centuries of overwhelming pain, especially for me, because my growth and development had been halted in all ways.

Our liberation was near, but we did not know that, and our lives continued as though we were floating in a sad sea of accumulated fatigue and weakness.

Until on May 8, between four and five in the morning, we learned that the Germans had abandoned the concentration camp and that we were free.

FREE, BUT NOT WHOLE

FREED FROM OUR HATEFUL NAZI CAPTORS, we ran toward the Russian troops that were marching toward the city. We ran until we reached a highway and then stopped in surprise. In front of us were tanks, armored cars, and a great many soldiers.

It is impressive to see a whole army arrive to peacefully occupy a city, without shooting or blood. And it was also impressive to see how the civilian population ran toward the troops, shouting and crying.

We eventually learned were in the city called San Georgenthal Sudetenland, which was located between Czechoslovakia and Hungary, and which no longer exists. One might think the entire population of San Georgenthal had turned out to meet the Russians, and they seemed to be in a state of hysteria.

Suddenly disconcerted and without knowing what to do, those of us who had fled the concentration camp remained immobile. Suddenly the front tank stopped and my mother ran toward it. A Russian officer handed her a piece of bread from the tank, and the armored car then renewed its march toward the city.

Having just come out of the concentration camp that morning, we were in a terrible state of fear and disorientation. Aside from the tank officer who gave the piece of bread to my mother, the Russians paid no attention to us even though it was evident that the majority of us urgently needed medical attention and all of us needed a good meal.

Confused, we all walked behind the soldiers, hoping someone would pay attention to us and help us. We were free, it is true, but our troubles had not ended.

A Tiny Refuge

We wandered in this way around the city, frightened, hungry, and ignored, until someone, we don't know who, advised the authorities about us and they at last took care of us. The municipal authorities divided us among the families of the city, ordering them to put us up and give us food.

Unfortunately, many of the women who were liberated with us died shortly afterward. Some died due to illness, and others died because they overate—trying to satisfy all their hunger too quickly. We never again saw many of our other companions and never knew what happened in their lives.

The lady of the house that took in my mother, sister, and me gave us an electric grill. With that, my mother prepared a vegetable soup without grease, and we slowly began to get our stomachs accustomed to new eating habits.

A week later we had recovered some of our strength although we were still emaciated, with sunken eyes and spirits full of sadness, fear, and uncertainty. But we were alive, and little by little we began to understand the significance of being free. Confused and frightened, we had not been out in the street since we had come into this Georgenthal house.

As we grew stronger, our desire to find out about my father and my brothers became more intense and more urgent. With growing uneasiness, we asked ourselves if they were alive and where they might be.

We decided it was time to leave this house and find a way to return home, if that were possible. My mother spoke to the lady of the house and told her we intended to return to our Hungarian village and wait for the possible return of the rest of our family.

"If you are really determined to go, your journey will not be at all easy," the woman told us. "The war has changed everything and almost all the trains are occupied by soldiers moving from one place to another. Moreover, you cannot travel dressed in those clothes and shod with those clogs. Allow me first to find you some clothes and appropriate shoes."

That good lady, as she had promised, supplied us clothing and shoes. With her help, we ceased to look like ex-concentration camp prisoners and our appearance improved considerably.

Multitudes on the Move

I do not remember exactly how we left San Georgenthal, but I remember we walked a lot and eventually managed to get on the roof of a railcar. The train was very slow. On the roofs of the railcars were soldiers, civilians, women, and children. It was an odd assortment of nationalities, ages, genders, all trying to get to home.

It was a colorful and dazzling spectacle to see the railway cars covered by all these people. Several times we descended from one train to board a different one, and sometimes we spent the whole night in a railway station to wait for the next train.

During the days and nights we traveled toward Budapest, we asked ourselves obsessively: Would we find Papa, Ernest, and Eugene? Would they still be alive? What had happened to them? What would happen to us if they didn't come back? Our doubts and worries tortured our minds.

Luckily, it was no longer cold as it was the middle of spring, and the days were cloudless and splendid. But as we traveled across the countryside, we witnessed the desolation of the villages and cities of Hungary.

The country had just come through an extremely violent war that destroyed many towns, left a countless number of houses in ruins, separated families, disrupted society, and saddened the spirit. The faces of the people were sad, angry, and afflicted. Men, women, and children everywhere appeared weak, hungry, poorly clothed, and desperate to find food and work or to reunite with someone dearly loved and feared lost forever.

The satisfaction of returning to our beloved homeland was marred by the tragedy of a destroyed country. And we still had no idea where my father and brothers were.

As we drew close to Budapest, I said to Mama, "We are about to reach our destination. Where are we going to sleep and who is going to give us food? Who will take care of us? From what we have seen from the train, there is a lot of misery everywhere."

My mother, with the admirable faith that never left her, told me confidently: "Don't worry, everything will be all right. Be sure that God is going to help us."

Between one train change and another, we were comfortably seated in a passenger car when we reached Budapest. When the train finally stopped at the railway station in the Hungarian capital, my heart began to beat faster. I am sure the same thing happened to my mother and Magdalena.

The station was filled by a human anthill. Crowds of people were anxiously scouring each arriving train for the possible arrival of their relatives. They interrogated incoming passengers, asking, "Do you know anything of such-and-such a family, native of X village?" A man stood on one of the platforms, shouting at the top of his lungs: "Do any of the arriving passengers know Mrs. Fulana, who lived in such-and-such a city?"

The majority of the arrivals, in turn, had many questions for the people waiting at the station. "We are the Z family. Do you know if anyone is waiting for us and has asked for us?" This kind of question was repeated a thousand times every time a train arrived.

A Voice Proclaims Joyous News

As my mother placed her foot on the first step to descend from the train, we heard a strong and clear masculine voice surging above the waves of noise from the multitude: "Margit, your sons and your husband are alive!"

There were so many people around us that we could not tell who had yelled this good news to Mama. But we went crazy with happiness, weeping, shouting, and embracing one another. Between smiles and sighs, my mother said to us: "You see how God heard me, my daughters; your father and your brothers are alive!"

At that moment I recovered my faith, that faith I had lost during our time in the Nazi concentration camps. I understood with sudden clarity that life had made us suffer greatly but that God also gave us great and good rewards. He had kept alive the beings who were blood of our blood and spirit of our spirits.

As we descended from the train into a crowd so thick we could hardly move, we desperately tried to locate the man who had shouted the good news to us. We knew it must have been someone from our village because he had called to my mother by name. We searched the station repeatedly but could not find a familiar face among the masses of people searching for their own familiar faces and asking questions of everyone.

Some time later, when we visited our village, we learned the identity of the good man who had called to my mother that my father and brothers were still alive. We were told this man had passed a whole month at the railway station in Budapest, even sleeping there, waiting and watching for any member of his family to arrive on one of the trains. But his wait was in vain because no one came back: not his wife, nor his children, nor his brothers or sisters. Absolutely no one.

Sadly enough he was not the only Hungarian to suffer such a tragedy. Thousands of men and women found themselves in the same situation. Entire families disappeared forever, without it even being known what place had received their remains. A long time would pass before the waiting ones finally accepted that their most-loved beings would not return. Their loved ones had been murdered. Some stubborn individuals never stopped waiting.

A Refuge in Beautiful Budapest

As we arrived at the railway station in Budapest, we saw some men who held signs high above the crowd so that they stood out among the sea of faces. These signs said something along the lines of: "All the survivors who are arriving should please pass to the waiting room."

After our unsuccessful search for the voice who had called out to Mama, we headed toward the waiting room, as the signs directed. One of the men in charge of attending to the returning survivors said to us: "I am going to take you to the JOINT for you to be registered. It is the only way those who were saved from death can find their relatives or be found by them. Maybe your names and place of origin are already listed there."

JOINT was the name of an international organization established after the Second World War in all the countries of Europe. Its purpose was to help survivors of the war and the concentration camps who were returning to their villages and cities. I understand this assistance program originated in the United States, which sent economic aid and food.

My mother, my sister, and I were registered in the book relating to the people of Szécsény. As the person who attended to us wrote down the surname Davidovich in the register, he said to us: "There is a lady living here in Budapest who comes to these offices daily to ask us if anyone has arrived by this name." He said her name was Mrs. Klein.

Full of emotion, my mother exclaimed, "It is my sister-in-law; please call her by telephone at once!"

When my aunt answered the call, she didn't want to waste time talking on the telephone to Mama so just told the JOINT employee that she was leaving at once to come and collect us.

When she arrived, the scenes of embraces, tears, and joy are indescribable. It was clear from the expression on her face that she found us very changed. At first, it was difficult for her to recognize us in our conditions: emaciated, sprouting six-centimeter long hair, and dirty, as we had no opportunity to bathe ourselves during the entire journey from Georgenthal to Budapest.

My aunt was very upset to see our deplorable state. The history of our suffering was eloquently written in our sunken eyes, our emaciated faces, and our undernourished bodies. She embraced us and wept, sad at our conditions but happy at having finally found us after many days of visiting the JOINT offices in Budapest.

The woman who came to collect us was the wife of my mother's brother who had a German silver factory in Budapest, which I mentioned in the early pages of this book. His factory made fruit stands, candelabra, candy dishes, trays, and other objects that were real works of art, comparable with the finest pieces of antique English silver.

In addition, my uncle, who had manufactured a German silver crown for the nation, was a veteran of the First World War. As an officer, he had been wounded in the leg in a battle, and he had been decorated twice: first by the army and then by the Hungarian government, which recognized the excellence of his industry and thanked him for the crown he had given to the nation.

My aunt explained the Hungarian government had protected him because of these decorations and did not hand him over to the Nazis. Because of the government protection, they managed to continue living in their house without being disturbed. Unfortunately, this uncle had died of a heart attack eight months ago, leaving my aunt a widow. She felt very lonely and was delighted to find us.

My aunt received us in her home with affection and warmth, while we waited for news of my father and my brothers. Day after day she accompanied us to the JOINT offices, where we waited anxiously for them to arrive. My aunt's address was already registered at JOINT so would be given to my father and my brothers when they arrived. But we were so anxious to see them and embrace them that we continued to visit JOINT every day.

My aunt lived in an attractive apartment in a very large house with an extensive patio. We lived with my aunt in her second-floor apartment with windows and glass doors looking out over the patio. There was a lovely antique fountain in the center of the patio, and the apartments were located around the patio, two floors high with a balcony running from one end to the other. It was one of the most beautiful buildings in the old part of Budapest.

RECONSTRUCTING
OUR FAMILY

ONE MORNING AT AROUND EIGHT O'CLOCK, I had washed my hands and was drying them next to one of the windows in my aunt's apartment when I glanced toward the patio and saw an old man, hunched over and wrapped in rags, carrying a small bundle on his back. He was reading a paper he held in his hand and looking all around him.

He looked again at the paper and once again glanced around. Without doubt he was trying to locate one of the apartments. I didn't pay much attention to him. A moment later I turned to leave the towel and again saw the same man still looking around. I decided I should help him, so I opened the door and called to him: "Sir, sir, what apartment number are you looking for!"

He lifted his eyes to me and I became paralyzed. Then I called out with all my strength: "It's my Papa!"

I could not move and stayed rooted to the spot with emotion. But my mother and my sister heard my cry and ran out toward the man. When I saw them, I ran too.

When Papa and Mama were face to face, they said nothing. Words were useless and insufficient. They simply wept while looking into one another's eyes. Then they embraced and sat down on the ground. Magdalena and I joined them and the four of us stayed there a good long time, sitting together and weeping.

Finally my mother asked between sobs: "And our sons?"

Papa responded only: "They are alive!" It was the first words he had spoken.

When we finally got up from the ground, we saw we were not alone. My aunt and the neighbors had all come out of their apartments when they heard me shout. They surrounded us and wept silently.

This scene of my father's return is engraved on the deepest part of my soul. Even now, forty years afterward, I feel a knot in my throat and tears come to my eyes when I remember it.

The Wait for My Brothers

When we were reunited with my father in Budapest he was forty-seven years old, but he looked as though he were seventy. He was excruciatingly thin and his hair had become completely white. His normal weight before the war had been 150 pounds, but when he returned he weighed only ninety pounds. A stoic and brave man, he told us nothing of his many sufferings during the year we were apart, but his physical state shouted that he had suffered in this time.

After we had returned to my aunt's apartment, Papa told us that he had been cruelly separated from my brothers many months before. We asked him what he meant by "cruelly," but he didn't want to talk more about the matter. When I was alone with my father, I demanded that he tell me everything, but he said, "You have all suffered greatly and it is neither fair nor pleasant to tell you of my sufferings, especially your mother, who is so worried about your brothers' absence."

After the liberation, my father had happened to run into a young man who had been a companion of my brothers in the place where they had been sent to do forced labor. This boy assured my father that my brothers were alive and told him they would doubtless return to our side in a few more days. Unfortunately, those few days became long and numerous, causing us much anxiety.

My father tried to calm us, encouraging us not to worry and telling us Ernest and Eugene would arrive when we least expected it. My mother, Magdalena, and I asked no more questions so we would not worry Papa more than necessary, but we exchanged tearful glances that showed we were haunted by the same question: "When will they return?"

Our painful wait lasted for two more weeks until my brother Ernest reached Budapest and immediately went to register at the JOINT offices. Papa and I went to those offices every day to see if there was any news for us. On that day, we were walking through one of the passageways of the building when we saw a young man with his back to us. His clothes were in tatters; he was dirty and his head had been shaved.

As he heard us approach, the young man turned his head. It was Ernest! Without a word, he threw himself into my father's arms, sobbing. He stayed there for a few moments before saying, in a voice choked with tears, "They took Eugene prisoner; the Russians captured him, mistaking him for a Hungarian soldier!"

The news left us speechless. Eventually I broke the silence and said, "But we are all alive, and we must thank God."

Then I ran to the telephone to let Mama know that Ernest had returned and was with us. But, how could I tell her about Eugene's absence and about his being captured by the Russians?

There was no alternative so I told her the truth. With her wonderful, steadfast faith, Mama said: "God will protect him."

Mistaken Identity

When my brothers were liberated from the Nazis by the Russians, they were at a place on the frontier between Hungary and Czechoslovakia. Those German soldiers who could escape fled from there; those who could not surrendered to the Russian troops.

Unfortunately, my brother Eugene was dressed well, so the Russians thought he was a soldier and took him as a prisoner of war. Eugene tried to explain that he was not a soldier, but the Russian soldiers could not understand his language so took him with the other captives.

Where had they taken Eugene? It was a mystery. Maybe to Siberia, where many of the soldiers captured by the Russians were taken. We knew nothing for a long time, and we would not be reunited with him for many more years.

Six months after the rest of my family had been reunited, we received a letter from Eugene that had been sent from Sebastopol, a Russian city located to the southwest of the Crimea. We later learned that he stayed there in a prisoner of war camp for a year before he was transferred to another POW camp at the port of Odessa in Ukraine. Being young and clever, Eugene learned the Russian language quickly. And as he was very clever with his hands, it occurred to him to make cigarette lighters using the wings of aircraft that had been shot down and to give them to the Russians, thus winning their sympathy. Thanks to these gifts, the Soviets who administered the prisoner of war camp grew to like him and gave him work in the kitchen. That assignment meant he ate well and did not suffer from cold during the winter season.

In 1948 Eugene was freed and went to Budapest, but our family had already left Hungary by then. Eugene married shortly after returning, and he tried to join us. But the new Hungarian government would not allow him to leave the country.

In 1956 there was an uprising in Hungary, during which much blood was spilled before Soviet troops put it down. It was a very painful episode, but it provided an opportunity for many young Hungarians to leave the country. Eugene and his wife managed to leave then and we were finally reunited after having been separated for thirteen years.

RETURNING TO AN
UNRECOGNIZABLE HOME

AFTER ERNEST WAS REUNITED with Papa, Mama, Magdalena, and me, we chose to return to our home in Szécsény. We knew there was no reason to wait in Budapest any longer for Eugene since he had been taken prisoner by the Russians.

We traveled to our village by train, arriving at our station around ten in the morning. The station was practically deserted with only one or two other people there. Our hearts were beating very fast and we were breathing erratically as we were overcome by a mixture of emotions, including nostalgia, anxiety, pain, and fear.

It took no more than ten minutes to walk from the railway station to Profeta Street. We saw no one we knew along the way, only numerous Russian soldiers on foot and on horseback. When we reached Profeta Street we realized the name had been changed to the Street of the Martyrs. And then we watched as an invisible knife was plunged into our parents' hearts.

The synagogue and our house were gone.

Where our house had been was only a vacant lot, covered with weeds that had grown to around four and a half feet high. Papa and Mama, with their hands linked, raised their eyes to the blue heavens of this clear and bright day, and cried "My God!" while the tears ran down their cheeks.

We began to search through the weeds, hoping to find a picture, a piece of furniture, or any object we could keep as a souvenir of what had been our family life in this now inhospitable and abandoned place.

To our sorrow, we found nothing.

We did not know what to do or where to go. What door could we knock at? Where could we find our old friends? Who could we ask for help? We were truly very much alone, destitute and sad.

My father, with his indomitable strength of character, managed to recover from this disappointment and say to us, "No matter, the important thing is that we are alive and together; let us see if the authorities can do anything for us."

The Szécsény authorities told my father we could occupy any house in the village which had belonged to a Jewish family but said we would have to share it with elements of the Russian Army. They advised him we would probably prefer to live with officers and not common soldiers, since the latter usually drank a lot and were disrespectful.

Disconcerted, my father said: "So I am going to move with my family into someone else's house? How am I going to tell the Russian officers that we want to share one of the houses with them? I don't even know them and cannot ask them that."

In order to make things easier for Papa, the village authorities decided to allocate to us one of the larger and better houses available.

Our Family's Rare Happy Fate

This house had belonged to a Jewish family with eight members; they had been well-off and good friends of ours. The family had been sent with us to Auschwitz but had not managed to survive. A common saying at the time was: "One enters Auschwitz through the door but comes out through the chimneys." The saying was very cruel, but that is how it was.

I want to note that our family was the only Jewish family I knew of that came back complete from the concentration camps. Of course, I am not talking about relatives outside of our six-person household because many brothers of my mother were exterminated, together with many cousins, nephews, and nieces.

The highest authority of the village took us to our assigned house. Before we crossed the enormous threshold, he told us, "The front part of this house consists of five rooms where you are going to live, and the rear part is occupied by Russian officers, who will not trouble you since the property is very large."

We settled in there with our hearts crushed, longing for our own house, which had disappeared. Once alone, my father said to us: "We are only here temporarily, and I hope that soon we can leave this place."

"But where can we go?" Mama asked him.

He replied: "Wherever. This house is not our home."

The following morning, at about six, I opened my eyes, looked around me and saw the room in which I had slept was flooded in the rays of a glorious reddish sun. Although the room was ugly and furnished only with two beds, I felt very well. We had a roof over our heads and we were free. Our breakfast that day was a piece of bread, which was all we had.

Later, a little fearfully, we went out into the garden of the house where we met our neighbors, the Russian officers. We found there was really no reason to fear them. They saluted us with great courtesy and, in their poor Hungarian, offered us coffee with milk. We gladly accepted, because we were very hungry.

One of the Russian officers asked Mama if she could prepare their daily meals, offering to pay her in food. She happily accepted, and in this way the problem of feeding her family was solved. From that day on, she cooked for the Russian officers, and they paid her with the same type of food that they ate.

One of our old servants, a peasant woman who had spent a long time in our house, found out we had returned to the village and came to see us. My mother had found her a husband, but she had lost him in the war. However, she told us she had some cows, so things were not going badly for her.

This good woman lived some eight kilometers from the village and asked my parents for permission to take me with her for a few days in order to supply me with good milk and cheese because I was very emaciated. I went with her for ten days.

She was very affectionate to me and had prepared a bed for me with good feather pillows and clean white sheets. She told me, "This bed is very humble, but I made it for you in the same way to which you were accustomed when I was serving in your house." She bathed me and put me to bed with the same affection she had shown me years before.

After ten days I returned to the side of my parents, a little healthier and with a load of milk and cheese from that good woman.

Finding Ways To Survive

Papa and my brother Ernest dedicated themselves to looking for work, whatever they could find. But our village was poverty-stricken; almost no one had the money or the means of earning a living. The war destroyed the economy of Szécsény and that of the whole country.

My sister helped Mama in the kitchen, and I decided to do something to help to support the family. I remembered there had been a man in the village who made waistcoats and jackets from sheepskin in a small workshop in his own home. I thought he might still be alive and went to look for him.

Luckily I found him in his small home workshop, working the same as always. On seeing me, he almost fainted and couldn't find the words to express himself. I asked, "Do you remember me?"

He was as frightened as though he had seen a ghost. Teeth chattering, he said, "But how is it you are alive?"

I asked, "Did you expect to see me dead?"

He replied, "The truth is yes, because I heard that they had killed all your family."

I explained that my family had managed to survive and that we had returned to the village.

He told me then that he was very glad to hear that we had been saved and asked, "What brings you to my house, child?"

I replied: "I want you to give me work in your shop. I know how to sew and can help you sewing waistcoats and jackets."

"But I have no money to pay you," he argued.

I said to him, "Don't give me money, pay me with food."

That seemed all right to him so we reached an agreement. I sewed the sides and the shoulders of the waistcoats, and he paid me weekly with a chicken, a little flour, and some oil. I worked in this small workshop until February 1946.

A Chance for a New Start

∾⤜⤏

WHILE WE LIVED IN THE HOUSE with the Russian officers in
Szécsény, my father worked to recover the identification documents
for the members of our family. He was trying to get things such as
birth certificates and marriage certificates—the basic indispensable
documentation for living in a society. But all his efforts were in vain.
The civil registry archives had disappeared, consumed in the fires
brought about by bombing raids during the war.

Papa and Mama also worked to remember the address of some of
my uncles, my mother's brothers, who had been living in Mexico for
several years. One day out of the blue, my mother suddenly remembered the address. She immediately wrote it down in order not to
forget it again.

Wasting no time, she sent her brothers this very brief telegram:
"We are alive, Reply."

Not long afterward we received a letter from these uncles, saying they were happy to know we had survived and inviting us to join
them in Mexico. Their offer made us very happy. The truth is there
was no longer any reason to stay in impoverished Hungary. Our only
remaining relative there was my aunt in Budapest, a person very
advanced in age who would never have wanted to leave that city.

Thus, we enthusiastically began to plan the voyage we had decided
to make.

By that time, ten more survivors had returned to our village. They
were solitary people, now without close family or distant, and seven of
them disappeared from Szécsény shortly after they returned. Each one
looked for a new and different destiny and we never saw them again.

We left Hungary toward the end of 1946, traveling to Vienna after passing through Czechoslovakia. Once we were in Vienna, my uncles in Mexico cabled us enough money to reach Paris. We were fearful during the whole journey because we had no identification papers. Luckily, no one asked for these documents during those days when we crossed various countries of post-war, devastated Europe.

I don't remember how long it took to reach the Austrian capital, nor how long we remained in that city. But I remember very well that we reached Paris by train at the beginning of December 1946.

Born Again in Paris

We sat on the benches of the Paris railway station while my father went to look for lodgings. He returned half an hour later to take us to a small hotel located a block from the station, at Gare L'Est 19, almost on the corner of Strasbourg Boulevard. This was called the Hotel Espalas, and it was looked after by the proprietor and his two daughters. As the three spoke German, it was easy for us to communicate with them.

Papa explained our difficult situation clearly to the hotel owner. We had no money or identification documents, but it was essential to advise our relatives in Mexico of our Paris address so they could help us. The hotel owner was very kind; he let us have three rooms and began to obtain all kinds of information for us.

He called the International Red Cross and the Paris Jewish community. At the Red Cross, with the information he provided, we were all issued documentation. The Jewish community, for its part, sent us to JOINT so we could eat there every day.

The owner of the hotel loaned Mama an electric grill and told her she could prepare our breakfast and supper in her room. That was how our life in Paris began, free and with great aspirations about going to Mexico. We had been born again; we were returning to life!

Shortly afterward we received letters from Mexico with the money necessary for us to live in Paris. Meanwhile, my uncles in Mexico were doing everything possible to arrange for our legal move to that country. It was not easy or quick; six months passed before our entry was authorized.

During those six months, we made contacts with the many people who joined us in the line each day in order to eat at JOINT. They all asked us questions, such as, "Where do you live and where are you planning to go?" Some replied with great sadness: "I have nowhere to go, they killed my family and all my relatives and I don't know where to go." Others said they were about to go to the United States, to Canada, to Palestine, to Australia. Every day we heard very painful and sad tales, and also a multitude of dreams, worries, and hopes.

Every week the five of us—Papa, Mama, Ernest, Magdalena, and I—went to the United States Embassy, since our documentation to travel to Mexico was to be sent there.

In order to pass the days, weeks, and months of the long wait, Papa took us to museums, for walks, to the gardens, and, on Sundays, to the Palace of Versailles. Paris is a very lovely city, the center of universal culture, but in all honesty, we could not fully enjoy its charm and attractions because of our constant anxiety about when we would receive the documentation which would allow us to leave and begin our new life.

Thank You, God

Finally, in May 1947, our documentation reached Paris through the U.S. Embassy. We were able to go to Mexico, a country which was then governed by Miguel Alemán Valdés, an extraordinary president of the country and an exceptional man who was good enough to sign the authorization allowing us to enter his country, which received us with open arms and allowed us to remake our lives.

To this head of the Mexican government, and to the then-Minister of Finance, the also deceased Ramón Beteta Quintana, who was also instrumental in making our legal entry to Mexico a reality, I render here the homage of my eternal gratitude.

Filled with emotion and extraordinarily happy, we began an air journey that took two days and allowed us to fly very high, close to God. We took advantage of our proximity to say, "Thank you, God."

We landed in Mexico at eight in the morning of May 24, 1947. At that moment, I knew that my name was Dina Davidovich. But I also knew that my old and painful identity, A-20102, would never be erased from my mind.

Epilogue

WHEN DINA AND HER FAMILY ARRIVED IN MEXICO in 1947, they faced yet another challenge—to rebuild a new life in an unfamiliar place and to build a life with the same warmth as the one they had been forced to leave. Although initially overwhelmed by the challenge, Dina learned to adapt to the culture and customs of her new home.

Most importantly, Dina recognized that she had been given a chance to fill her life with opportunities, which, not long before, had seemed unlikely. She saw her new situation in a new country as a "return to life," a mindset reflected in every step she would take for the rest of her days.

Eventually, Dina fell in love, got married, and became a mother to four beautiful children. She took immense pride in motherhood, watching her children grow up and embark on their own journeys across the United States and Canada. Dina also developed a love for travel, which allowed her to frequently visit the family she cherished so deeply and surround herself with the loving future she had fought so hard for.

In 1985, on the fortieth anniversary of her liberation, Dina felt that it was time to share her story of survival with the world. She published her book in both Hungarian and Spanish and became widely recognized for her grit and resilience. Dina's story even found its way back to her hometown, Szécsény, and she was honored there with keys to the city as a symbol of appreciation for her tireless perseverance and courage.

Across the world, a school in Costa Rica produced a play based on Dina's book, and she was flown there to attend the performance. These moments, along with many others, stood as a testament to how far Dina had come in her life and to the legacy she was building for generations to follow.

In 2006, at the age of seventy-five, Dina passed away peacefully in her sleep at her home in Mexico City. But her memory lives on in the hearts of her children, grandchildren, and great-grandchildren, who owe their existence to her strength in the face of darkness.

In 2021, Dina's family witnessed the frightening parallels between the growing rates of antisemitism around the globe and the rise of antisemitism in Nazi Germany as described in Dina's testimony. Inspired by a more solidified understanding of the book's necessity in our current world, they began working to translate and publish *Return to Life* in English in order to further amplify Dina's words.

Today, her descendants continue to tell her story as they fight to ensure that the world never forgets what happened to Dina and the millions of others who endured the Holocaust.

Dina's parents, Ignacio and Margit Davidovich, in the 1970s in Mexico City. They were 75 years old in this picture.

After Dina published Return to Life *in Hungarian, she was honored in her hometown, Szécsény, for her perseverance and courage.*

Dina and her siblings in August 1986 during a presentation of Return to Life *in Spanish. From left, Eugene, Dina, Ernest, and Magdalena.*

Dina's children and her nieces and nephews at a gathering in Costa Rica in 1990. Top row: Julie and Burton; second row from left: Roberto, Tomas, Manuel, Henry, Rita, Roxana, Luis, and Ricardo; bottom row: Rosa. Manuel, Rita, Luis, and Rosa are Dina's children.

Dina visits the Hungarian Embassy in Mexico City in 2004. Although she lived most of her life in Mexico, Dina was always proud of her Hungarian roots.

Dina with her children and their spouses in 2002. From left, Manuel; Pam and Luis; Dina; Larry and Rosa; and Rita and Pepe. Manuel, Luis, Rosa, and Rita are Dina's children.

Dina with five of her grandchildren in 2002. Standing with Dina is Idan. Seated are (from left) Ingrid, Ricky, Alec, and Ashley. Idan and Ricky are the children of Dina's oldest son, Luis. Alec is the son of Dina's youngest son, Manuel. Ingrid and Ashley are the children of Dina's youngest daughter, Rosa.

Dina's daughter Rita (middle) in 2023 with her children, Eduardo (top left) and Katia (top right); and grandchildren, Mateo (top center), Dena (middle left), Ayden (middle right), and Solvi (bottom). Rita, Dena, and Eduardo have worked to publish Dina's story in English because they want the world to remember Dina and the millions like her who were swept up in the horrors of the Holocaust.

About the Author

DINA DAVIDOVICH was an author, speaker, and Holocaust survivor from Széchény, Hungary. Born in 1931, young Dina enjoyed the safety and beauty of her small Hungarian village, as well as the amity across those of religious and cultural diff erences. However, this tranquility would be tragically and abruptly cut short by the growing anti-Semitism in Europe at the time. At just thirteen years of age, Dina along with her mother and older sister were forcefully taken to multiple Nazi concentration camps over the course of a year as part of Hitler's desperate last gasp toward the end of World War II. In the darkest moments, Dina never gave up her fi ght for life, surviving the infamous six-day "Death March" before fi nding herself liberated by the Red Army in 1945. On the fortieth anniversary of her unlikely emancipation, Dina's impulse to tell her story led her to write the powerful testimony that became *Return to Life*. Dina lived out the rest of her life in Mexico City, Mexico, surrounded by her children and grandchildren—the truest testament of life. Although she passed away at the age of seventy-fi ve in 2006, Dina's message still rings loud and true: all hate needs to persist is for humanity to remain silent. We must never forget.

Made in the USA
Las Vegas, NV
07 May 2025